Time to Eat

Healing Mind, Body, and Soul
with a Modern-day Macrobiotic Lifestyle

The Story of a Once-Starved Survivor

Christina Campion

Fulton Books
Meadville, PA

Published by Fulton Books 2022

ISBN 979-8-88505-189-7 (paperback)
ISBN 979-8-88505-190-3 (digital)

Printed in the United States of America

Within each of us exists all the information of the entire universe. But we have either forgotten it and/or it is blocked or stuck deep within our DNA cells due to all the generational afore years of inappropriate diets and lifestyles that took us further and further away from our most natural and divine source of knowledge and knowing.

To the great good health and well-being of all sentient beings and our magnificent planet Earth.

I was happy to guide Christina and be part of her journey to health. I always admired her courage and tenacity in following everything to completion. This is the spirit that always leads to lasting health.

—Denny Waxman

Denny Waxman is a senior macrobiotic counselor, teacher, and author of *The Great Life Diet, The Complete Macrobiotic Diet and The Ultimate Guide to Eating for Longevity.*

Denny is the founder of the Strengthening Health Institute (SHI) Philadelphia, Pennsylvania.

Contents

Introduction

Half Starved

I had been away for three months, and when I returned, my husband said, "You look like death." I hadn't looked at myself in a mirror naked until then, and I was so deeply shocked at how malnourished I looked. And suddenly, I was very afraid. I had turned from a healthy, full-fleshed young woman into a near skeleton.

This is the story of how I almost died of starvation and malnutrition from an eating disorder. I am writing this very intimate story in the hope that it may help others improve their health. My condition had such complex origins that came to include multiple diagnoses, and many readers may very well identify with one or more of my afflictions.

On my last day of boarding school in 1972, an accidental food regurgitation incident caused me to become generally fearful of food and eating and triggered a pattern of behavior that would plague me for the next thirteen years.

From that day forward, I struggled on and off with both acute and chronic anorexia, bulimia, and some alcohol-dependency. I also experimented with some psychedelic drugs and various alternative dietary, fasting, and cleansing programs, eventually embracing wholeheartedly and with great naivete and ignorance, a macrobiotic diet and lifestyle.

However, the ignorance of my condition and lack of understanding of which dishes and how best to prepare them for that condition slowly but surely got me into a real pickle until in the autumn of 1989 when, at 5'7" and weighing only seventy-eight pounds, it became clear that if help were not found soon, I would probably die.

Thankfully, that help came in the form of some commonsense advice given by a senior macrobiotic counselor. The dietary and life-style changes that he recommended and periodically adjusted thereafter saved my life, and as I began to heal on many different levels, I started to understand more clearly the nature of this oftentimes life-threatening disease.

I have chosen to include, in particular, all the different food and drink-related experiences because they surely give reference to my condition, life journey, and vocational interest in both what I was fed and my food choices. My search eventually led to a more healthy, intuitive place.

I have met and studied with some extraordinarily wise and evolved teachers and have been guided to use some interesting tools, including yoga, shiatsu, aikido, tai chi, macrobiotics, do-in, tantra, and nine-star ki. They have all been, without a doubt, slowly but surely helping me to heal on many levels and to know and become who I am and my purpose in this lifetime.

I do not think of myself as a writer, preferring to be more physically active and unable to keep myself pepped up with caffeine, which seems to be the common writers' friend, finds me very challenged to have taken on this task. In addition, as a highly sensitive and rather private person who shies away from attention, I prefer instead to be a quiet observer, listener, and reader.

However, I simply haven't had and don't have a say or choice in the matter, though, as it, the book, seems to have chosen me.

During the summer of 1993, I received a strong message that I needed to start writing an account of my life experiences with food and eating, and ever since, this inner voice has been urging me forward, sometimes gently reminding but more often insisting with urgency.

In the past year, this voice grew especially loud, and at last, unable to ignore it any longer, I was called to the task of finishing this book.

I had thought I would need to be in a very quiet and secluded setting in order to make the final push but found myself in a fairly busy, oftentimes noisy and stressful, urban, albeit tropical, setting for the five months that I allotted to write. The saving grace was being located a mere five-minutes' walk to a beautiful beach on the south shore of Maui, Hawaii, where I walked and swam almost daily. This definitely helped the progress.

Chapter 1

The Roots of the Problem

Saying that a large percentage of the world population suffers from some type of eating disorder, alcohol, obsessive-compulsive, and/or drug dependency will probably come as no great surprise to many people. Moreover, the chances are that many readers of this book may have gone or are indeed even now going through an uncomfortable food, drug, or behaviorally compulsive-related experience and/or know someone who is.

What might be of some news and interest is that these diseases—commonly known today as anorexia, bulimia, obesity, and behavioral and drug addictions—are all symptoms of an underlying condition of *hypoglycemia*.

I was born with this condition.

Now thirty-two years later, I wish to share the account of how my expansive inquiry into achieving good health eventually guided me to use a natural plant-based diet and lifestyle and a simple format that helped me better understand and heal this hypoglycemic birth condition. Furthermore, it seems that very few people are able to see or make the connection of eating disorders, addictions, and drug dependency with this very worldwide prevalent disease, and I attempt to explain how simply it can be addressed, helped, and healed.

Why do I call my story *Time to Eat?*

The title has its origins in my childhood when my siblings and I went to live with our maternal grandmother. Mealtimes were strictly adhered to, and yet the meals themselves were rushed and tense. It was as if there was *no* time to eat with disastrous results. Then years later, I experienced for the first time in my life what it felt like to eat consciously and slowly and to truly take time to eat, especially at regular times. Hence, this very meaningful title.

Mealtimes at Saint Nicholas, the home of my grandparents:

A large, Asian, brass, carved gong or brass bell was rung by one of the house staff when it was time for a meal. These times were set in stone from generations past and only lapsed as the staff either died or left, and the formality of the gong or bell dropped, though lunchtimes remained at 1:00 p.m. Then no time to eat. This wreaked havoc on my nervous system and the already compromised inner organs.

I totally understand that the staff needed to be considered, though we often had to help with setting the tables, clearing plates, and in later years, washing up afterward. I am so very grateful to my grandmother for instilling in me a sense of regularity around mealtimes, which would later serve to help me heal. Also and especially that I was taught these manners of being helpful and considerate. This routine at Saint Nicholas went on daily for years until finally, as funds diminished, there wasn't even a cook to cater to those mealtimes.

My grandmother was born in a 120-room castle in 1901 (Lumley Castle, near Durham, was the seat of her father and mother, the Tenth Earl and Countess of Scarborough). She was raised by a series of mostly very strict, cold-hearted, older spinster governesses. She saw her parents for thirty minutes daily at 4:00 p.m. (tea time) and only if they were in residence, as they constantly moved in between their various other stately homes in England (one of which was at 21 Park Lane in London that was bombed during World War II and on which foundation the London Hilton now stands).

My grandmother told me her childhood was quite miserable, and she vowed that when she grew up, she would always try and surround herself with loving people for the rest of her life. And she managed to fulfill that promise. She had a premonition at age twelve years that she would marry my grandfather after his first wife (sister of her father) died, and so she did in 1922. I still have her engagement dress and silk-embroidered shawl, both of which I have worn on several occasions!

She tried really hard to be a wonderful, modern, up-to-date grandmother and succeeded in various ways, but on the other side, she would become rather nasty when crossed, and if she felt she was losing control with any of us four grandchildren, she would dole out punishments similar to those given to her as a child.

She said my grandfather accepted the fact that she was thirty years younger and still had needs that he was unable to meet and so he turned a blind eye to her extramarital goings-on, and she was always very discreet. GP apparently adored and supported her in all her ways.

Chapter 2

My Early Life: Food Memories

I was born in a private clinic near Newcastle upon Tyne, Northumberland, England, on Tuesday, June 4, 1957, and although the exact time is unknown, according to my father's poetic words, "daylight was in the sky when she took her first breath." I was the second child of what would eventually become a family of four children: three girls and the youngest, a boy.

Simply put, as a newborn, I was unable to accept food initially because of the condition of my internal organs. I have come to understand that my spleen and pancreas, the organs necessary for producing and supplying the blood with insulin, which feed the brain to survive and evolve, were severely compromised and constricted. I was finally tempted to eat when my grandmother intervened and insisted I be given an extremely rich sweet food traditionally given to babies that were either premature, malnourished, or somehow not thriving and consisted of raw, unpasteurized, full-cream cow's milk generously laced with white sugar. This formula served to create an ever-increasing dependency, which over time, exacerbated and further weakened those organs.

(A shocker: Additional information came to me fairly recently on the subject of the family alcohol dependency. In 2012, my father wrote an article for a local newspaper in Bhurmannsdriff, South Africa, where he was living and sent out copies to all his five children. He basically said that he was tired of hearing so many new parents complaining about what a hard time they were having getting their babies to settle and that they, the families, were all sleep deprived. Dad said that he had used a simple solution. Both he and my mother had a snifter of brandy before bedtime, and they topped off the baby bottles with the same brandy, insuring the whole family slept through the night and woke up refreshed and ready for the new day.)

This first alcoholic "nourishment" added an extra layer to the platform of the next thirty-two years of my life, which were spent for the most part struggling to maintain balance in a body that rarely seemed to be functioning normally and eventually brought me to the brink of death.

Webster's definition of the word *anorexia* as a noun is "a loss of appetite; inability to eat" and *anorexia nervosa* "an eating disorder primarily affecting adolescent girls and young women, characterized by a pathological fear of becoming fat, distorted body image, excessive dieting, and emaciation."

The more commonly held viewpoint and diagnosis of a person who refuses to eat is that they have anorexia nervosa.

In the case of a newborn baby who rejects nourishment, the latter is not applicable. Most living beings have a strong survival instinct, and the only factor that would override that would be the inability to act on that instinct or not be offered food that would be life enhancing or create balance.

I do not remember much of those first four years of my life, although certain moments and events are as clear as if they happened yesterday. Our first home in Newcastle was a two-story flat, and I only remember a single instance in which I was there. I was upstairs with my elder sister in the evening, peering through the loft-landing banister to the downstairs area where our parents were sitting with some visiting cousins.

In 1958, around the time of my younger sister's birth, we moved from Newcastle to a small village on the outskirts of Leeds, West Yorkshire, and during the next three years, I had a few eating-related memories.

I remember sitting in a high chair with a mouthful of tinned peas, which I refused to swallow. How do I know they were tinned peas? The memory of this taste was triggered repeatedly throughout my childhood and adolescence. Nowadays, I actually rather like the taste of some tinned peas, particularly *petit pois*.

I also recall staying with my maternal grandparents to be potty trained, having only just recently begun to walk. On one occasion, I was outside their house walking toward my grandfather, GP, whose arms were outstretched, beckoning me to him, as my grandmother took a photograph from behind. I know this to be true as the photograph still exists. One day, GP showed me how to eat a pear properly. He cut the fruit in half lengthways and then using a teaspoon, carefully scooped out the seed area and then proceeded to scoop the fruit out, leaving an empty shell of skin. Another time when we were having strawberries for lunch, he showed me that he liked to dip his strawberries into the little pile of salt that he had placed on his plate instead of the sugar and cream that my grandmother enjoyed. I tried them both and of course, preferred the sweet, creamy taste. When GP was in his last months of life, he spent most of his days in bed in the dressing room adjacent to their marital bedroom, and I remember climbing into his bed in the mornings and sharing his breakfast of "bud and butta," fresh white bread and the home-farm butter along with some hot milk.

I remember often lying on the sofa in the sitting room in our West Yorkshire home while a dark-suited doctor inserted, what I later learned was a suppository, into my bum—the resulting remedy of the chronic constipation I suffered since birth.

Chapter 3

Dramatic Changes

Sometime in early January 1962, I was sitting on the banister at the top of the staircase when my father appeared dressed in a suit and overcoat and carried a large suitcase. I said, "Hello, daddy," and asked him where he was going and then slid down the handrail as he walked down the stairs. He picked me up, hugged me, and said he was going away but that I was his favorite little girl and he loved me very much.

That was the day my father walked out of our home to go and live with another woman, never to return, and my mother was left with her four children ages six, four, three, and three months. She struggled to take care of us all on her own for a few days but had what was called back then a nervous breakdown and was taken to a private nursing home/sanitarium where she stayed for almost a year and a half, and we did not see her during all that time.

Life took a very different direction from then on, and after spending some time with our aunt, we all then went to live with our maternal grandmother, whom we endearingly called MM—short for mummy's mummy.

Our new home was a forty-room, stone dower house situated on the outskirts of a historic town on the edge of the North Yorkshire moors. The original house was a farmhouse built in 1113 but renovated several times, once after a big fire. At one time, it became a hospice ran by monks and was dedicated to Saint Nicholas, the patron saint of children, and is still called that today. It is surrounded by seven acres of semiformal gardens (that had all been planted from seeds and cuttings by my grandfather, GP), fields, woodlands, and a farm complete with a working dairy, cows, sheep, pigs, hens, and various crops and totaled over two hundred acres. At the time of our arrival, the whole estate was cared for by many full-time and some other part-time staff, who lived on or near the estate and included a cook, housekeeper, cleaning maid, chauffeur, head gardener, and tenant farmer and his family, although there had been triple the staff before the Second World War.

My grandfather had died earlier that year, and his empty dressing room was fitted with three more beds and all four of us children moved in. My brother was in a cot until old enough to graduate to a bed. My grandmother made us all take turns in a different bed once a week when the sheets were changed. Two of the beds had horsehair mattresses, and the other two were modern foam/sprung ones, so naturally, we had very different sleeping experiences as the rotation moved us onto the next bed.

Chapter 4

Life with MM

My grandmother was a beautiful aristocratic lady who was born in 1901. She was very social both within her family circle and the surrounding community and seemed to be constantly in a hurry and busy, even when sitting down. She was loving but strict and had little or no tolerance for those who disobeyed her or were slow or lagged behind. She scolded harshly and liberally doled out punishment in order to control us.

My father had initially been given monthly visiting rights and would come on allotted weekends to take us out for the day, and I remember that at the end of these days out with Dad we were all crying our eyes out, not wanting him to go. This caused an extra stress on my grandmother, and she eventually got the family court to end his visitation rights. I would not see my father again until I was twelve years old. He stayed in touch by sending us all presents on birthdays and holidays, but his name wasn't mentioned much.

Life with MM seemed to revolve around a very set format with punctuality for mealtimes being a top priority. They were always at a regular fixed time, and in those days for us children, breakfast was at 8:00 a.m., lunch was the main meal of the day at 1:00 p.m., and a very light supper at 6:00 p.m. Evening dinner was served for adults and house guests at about 8:00 p.m.

In the mornings, when not at school, we were sent into the garden to pick vegetables and/or fruits for the cook and asked to help both the cook and housekeeper in the kitchen and with the washing up of dishes after lunch. Meals were announced by the housekeeper, June, hitting a gong, and being late into the dining room was not tolerated by MM. She would be furious and most often doled out some punishment, which usually meant that one didn't get to have the after-lunch sweet treat. However, even though MM insisted on us being in the dining room on time, once there, she rushed us all to finish quickly, and even though it was time to eat, there was no time to eat and enjoy the food. All the meals consisted of vast quantities of very rich animal food that was usually cooked in the beef or pork drippings (i.e., lard). A variety of different kinds of meat and potatoes were daily fare as were dairy and homegrown vegetables that were boiled to death with lots of salt and generous amounts of farm butter. Certain dishes were usually served on certain days—i.e., roast beef with Yorkshire pudding and gravy was always served on Sundays, liver and onions on Mondays, lamb chops with mint sauce on Tuesdays, minced meat with onions and fried bread on Wednesdays, roasted wild fowl like grouse or pheasant on Thursdays, some local caught fish was always served on Fridays, and curry made from the leftover chicken of the week might be served on Saturdays. Rich steamed and baked puddings and cooked and fresh fruits that were always served with thick cream and white or soft, brown sugar were also served daily.

Sweeties (candy) and lump sugar were given after lunch unless anyone had misbehaved, which more often than not was me. Most of what we ate came from the tenant-run home farm and garden, though as time went by and the staff dwindled, produced less. We all had to take a nap after lunch, and after that, we had to take a walk for one hour, often staying on the estate and going over to the farm to see the animals and find some eggs in the hayloft. We were allowed to take turns helping to churn the milk into butter and given some of the slightly sour-tasting whey, which was called pig's milk because it was fed to the pigs. I loved those trips to the farm and especially when there were newborn calves, piglets, lambs, or hatched chicks. On the way back, we had to gather dry kindling for the wood-burning fires. The eggs we had collected were soft boiled for supper and served with hot buttered toast soldiers that we dipped into the rich yolks.

We girls were all dressed alike until we started to assert our own unique tastes. We all had identical clothing and indoor and outdoor shoes. Before going up to bed, we had to line up these shoes at the bottom of the stairs to be found in the morning in the dining room cleaned and polished by the chauffeur / valet / butler / hedge trimmer, Mr. Smith.

Mr. Smith was a very wonderful person—my grandmother had found him in London where he was lighting gas lamps outside their London house on Park Lane (that was bombed during the war a few years later), and she invited him and Mrs. Smith to be employed and come and live up in Yorkshire. We would often stop in on the Smiths in the morning and have a midmorning snack with them consisting of biscuits and a soda drink called Dandelion and Burdock. This drink was Mr. Smith's favorite beverage and the original root beer and forerunner to Coca-Cola and Pepsi. Little did I know that years later, dandelion and burdock would become two of my favorite vegetables.

From the start, my grandmother seemed to be especially annoyed and frustrated with me. My naturally slower pace, generally weakened immune system, and especially my chronic constipation were very upsetting to her. She insisted that I have a poo each morning after breakfast and ordered me to make this happen and if not, I would not get the chocolate bar treat that we all were given on Sunday. So I would push and strain, and sometimes my eyes would become bloodshot from the effort, which may or may not have produced something to show her.

When I had not performed for a couple of days, she would dose me with a ghastly tasting medicine called syrup of figs, which sometimes had no effect, so she would then give a double dose. On one such occasion, I awoke, crying, in the night in a pool of diarrhea. My grandmother was furious to be woken up to this and very roughly put me in a lukewarm bath to wash me off (the hot water was not on at night) and then put me back in the bed minus fresh sheets and only the all-wool, itchy blankets for cover.

This was the tail end of a previous punishment that consisted of anyone who misbehaved being put in a separate bedroom, and I was in such a room that night. The worst room, though, was the night nursery one. That part of the house had been added on prior to my aunt and mother's arrival and never seemed to ever get warm in spite of the fact that most of the house was heated by hot water fed into radiators in each room, including the lavatories. And there was also a fireplace in every bedroom and the downstairs living rooms. However, after GP died, MM let some of the staff go and became frugal with the heating system. The housemaid put hot water bottles in each of the beds to warm them up, and I remember often climbing into a bed that was wet from the condensation that had formed.

One time when we were all in GP's room, my elder sister awoke crying as her hot water bottle had burst in the bed and it was soaked. She got to go downstairs and had hot chocolate by the fire, and I decided I would undo my hot water bottle so that I might get the same treat—big mistake. I was spanked, scolded, and made to sleep once again in sheetless, itchy wool blankets.

It seems that all through my childhood, I was constantly ill, and this continued into adolescence. I remember the pain of chronic and acute toothaches, earaches, reoccurring sore throats, and a whooping-like cough along with all the then-common childhood diseases of mumps, chickenpox, measles, and German measles.

I had my first dental experience when I was five years old—sitting in the family dentist's chair, one of those big black leather ones. The smell in the room was strongly antiseptic, stimulating, and made me feel rather light-headed. The nurse put a rubber mask over my nose and mouth and gassed me for the extraction of a baby molar tooth that had gone bad. The sensation was so strange as I slipped away into a magical floating dreamworld until I heard the dentist's voice in the distance saying my name and bringing me back. I was given a glass of pink water to rinse my mouth and a little envelope of some of the pink-making antiseptic tablets to take home. This was the beginning of seemingly endless visits to the dentist, as my teeth decayed rapidly.

A young Chinese dentist who had moved to the town with his wife and children started to assist our elderly family dentist in the practice. He and his family were obviously very out of place in this old-fashioned, racist Yorkshire place. So much so that one weekend, when the office was closed, he committed suicide in that black leather chair that I was so accustomed to sitting in.

Whenever I was ill, I was put in a separate bedroom and usually the one that was called the dressing room (so called as it was a small room adjoining a master bedroom). That bedroom had two still-life paintings of fruit and dead chickens, whose heads were hanging over the edge of the table on which they were placed. There was also a large French window that opened onto a veranda that could be walked on and had a wonderful view of the driveway in front of the house with the fields and the ancient Abbey ruins far off in the distance. Once, I climbed out to explore, and wouldn't you know it, in came MM, the angry voice, and inevitable scolding and spanking.

All day long, I craved sweets and sugar and remember often sneaking back into the breakfast dining room to get a piece of leftover toast, which I would butter and then heap on a generous amount of homemade marmalade. I remember the feeling of how nice it was to eat this alone and quietly because mealtimes were so rushed and such a battleground when MM would scold or find fault with me and I could never eat quickly enough for her liking.

"Hurry up and finish what's on your plate or you won't get pudding." I was a skinny child, and she would often remark on this, but if I asked for seconds, she would call me greedy. I think I can say, without a doubt, that from a very young age, I was confused and uncomfortable in my body.

I do remember one of the special things that MM used to do for me and my sisters. The night before a party or special event, our hair were washed and then we were allowed to go downstairs to the coziest room in the house called the smoking room (where smoking was allowed) and MM would very skillfully roll sections of our long, wet hair up in cotton rags in order to make curls or waves. We then got to sit in front of the fireplace to dry it. It was fun to wake up in the morning and take out the rags to find lovely waves in my normally straight long hair.

Many mornings, MM would take us all with her to the nearby town of Richmond to do the shopping. She would often buy a loaf of fresh white bread (brown/whole wheat bread didn't come onto the scene until many years later) and then leave us all in the car with a square of farm butter and a knife to eat this delicious hot fresh bread while she did the shopping.

After a year at Saint Nicholas, a new modern house was beginning to be built at the top end of the garden next to the tenant cottages so that we could all live nearby with Mum when she was discharged from the nursing home. The arrangement was that we would live with Mum during the school week and then go down the garden to grandmother at weekends and during school holidays. This was my grandmother's way of lessening the load on my mother of suddenly being a single mother to four young and rather-high-spirited children.

Soon after we moved into the new house, I started to have a recurring nightmare. In it, I would feel myself floating upward to the sky and beyond with white billowy clouds, which turned into white linen-clad pillows and there was a strange sensation of contraction and expansion. One minute I was tiny and then the next minute, huge. This really frightened me, and I awoke crying and sweating. I would climb out of the upstairs bunkbed that I shared with my younger sister and sit halfway down the staircase crying until Mum would hear and come to comfort me and she would then put me into her bed for the night.

I also started to have the chronic sore throats that appeared almost every six weeks, during which time I would have a high temperature and be unable to swallow or talk and would usually be in bed for a week or more. I became a guinea pig for the new antibiotic, penicillin. This was given in the form of a very sweet, thick, pink, strawberry-flavored liquid. I remember eating a lot of fresh oranges mostly consumed by sucking the juice out because it was too painful to swallow anything remotely fibrous or solid. It was suggested that my tonsils needed to be removed, but luckily for me, MM didn't believe in those kind of extreme remedies, and thanks to her, I still have them intact.

My immune system was further compromised with the regular rounds of antibiotics, and when I was nine, I suddenly developed an itchy, sore rash on my hands and back that stayed for almost two years. I would spend many hours rubbing my back against the edge of a doorway in an effort to appease the itch. The family doctor gave me various creams to apply for this condition for which he could offer no explanation. He thought only that I may be allergic to the geraniums or some other plant in the house, and I was told not to touch them. Bandages covered my hands, mainly to prevent my further irritating the rash.

School holidays were spent in the company of relatives who would either stay with us at Saint Nicholas or we would travel to stay with them in various parts of the British Isles. On one of those first holidays with MM, she took us by train, car, ferry, and car again to stay with an old widowed relative, Sally, in Annestown, County Waterford, in Southern Ireland. (I think the population of Annestown back then in 1965 was about six people, and as I write this, there are only twenty-five cottages.) Sally was a very gifted artist and lived in a dear little cottage just across the road from the beach. We went shrimping with shrimp nets in the early evenings, and Sally deep-fried them along with very thinly sliced potato rounds for supper. She also gave us delicious homemade cakes. Several years later, Sally (along with two other elderly relatives) came to live out her last years at Saint Nicholas and spent much of that time painting.

One time, MM took us to Cornwall on the Southwest corner of England, and we were introduced to Cornish tea, which is hot-buttered scones with homemade strawberry jam and clotted cream, which to this day still makes me smile thinking about it because of its rich sweetness. It was on that trip that I was allowed to buy my first bikini swimsuit, a flimsy little two-piece made from a delightful burgundy-patterned cotton.

I especially loved the trips to the Highlands of Scotland, staying in the guesthouse of a beautiful old estate house that had burned several years back. Those summer days were spent roaming in the heather hills, riding horseback with neighbors, rowing the boat on the estate's loch (lake), watching the oil lamps being lit at dusk, and because the air was so clean and we were high up in the mountains, going to bed at 7:00 p.m. and sleeping till 7:00 a.m. the next day. I felt a freedom up there that I carried with me as a reference for where and how I wanted to live later on in my life.

Chapter 5

Day School and Queen Margaret's Boarding School

We were all given private educations and at different ages were sent off to various mostly non-coed boarding schools around the United Kingdom. The years spent at the local day school that I attended for five through eleven years holds one strong food memory in the form of the half-pint bottle of full-cream milk with its thick layer of cream on the top that we were given every day for a midmorning snack.

When I was eight years old, I remember the English teacher in this day school telling our class that the sprouts of potatoes caused cancer and we should therefore probably best avoid them. I announced at lunch on the following weekend that I would not be eating potatoes again. I think I wasn't too strict about it as I do remember enjoying crisps (potato chips) and french fries. Interestingly enough, about two years later, I decided to stop eating meat. MM was not amused and said I would starve to death. She insisted that I have cheese to make up for the lack of protein, and I was fine with that. Many years later, I would begin to understand how all these conscious choices and changes were in part due to and would affect my underlying root condition of hypoglycemia.

I had joined the Brownies (and later Girl Guides) with my best friend, Kay, who lived close to us on the same road. Once when we were all staying at Saint Nicholas for Christmas, I remember

17

quite vividly stealing loose change from the purse in Mum's handbag, which was on the chair in the dressing room bedroom (the one with the dead chickens paintings), and using it to buy sweets from the shop that Kay and I would go into on the way back from the Brownies's meetings that we walked to and from each week. Such were my cravings for sugar all through my childhood and which became greater as the years passed. I had no real interest in any other foods, except cream, butter, and anything fatty. At Christmastime and birthdays when traditional fruitcake with icing and marzipan was served, I would happily eat all the icing and marzipan off the cake and swap the fruitcake with those who didn't want their icing or marzipan for all that might be left on their plates.

During the summer holidays of 1968, just after my eleventh birthday, my monthly periods started. It happened whilst my younger sister and I were traveling via sleeper car on a train bound for Wiltshire to go and stay with cousins in the South of England. I knew very little and other than having seen my elder sisters' sanitary tampons and pads, had not been told much about the natural cycles and changes that a girl would experience and how to manage them. Coupled with being introverted, I remember feeling very embarrassed and yet excited at this new stage of my life, but I was unable to speak about it with anyone until I next saw my mother a few weeks later. I stole a tampon from the room of the nanny employed by the cousins with whom I was staying but being unable to insert it, flushed it down the lavatory and instead used many folded sheets of lavatory paper. Cousin P commented one day that "you girls certainly use a lot of loo paper," and I died a thousand deaths.

I had my first introduction to tasting cooked seaweed when I spent a week helping cousin P the following year as her live-in mother's helper at their family summer house in coastal Cornwall. We went to the beach for a picnic lunch, and Cousin Phil said she had heard that seaweed had a lot of iron and she wanted to try eating some. So we gathered some of the seaweed that had been washed up the night before and cooked it on a little camping stove in fresh water. It had an interesting flavor but was very fishy, and we laughed a lot at the experience. However, years later, several varieties of cooked seaweed became and are still, to this day, a vital and delicious part in my daily cooking and diet.

My elder sister had been sent to a Russian ballet boarding school when she was eight years old, so I rarely saw her. When I did see her, the stories she told me of her life at school sounded so fun and exciting and I begged to be able to join her there. Not being inclined toward ballet as she was, I was eventually sent to an all-girls boarding school near the City of York about an hour away from home. I was excited by the preparations that were made in the buying and making (Beth, the cook, sewed many of our clothes) of the required school uniform and the packing of the trunk as we marked off the items on the list provided. We were allowed to take three changes of home clothing to be worn only after supper on weekdays, Saturdays, and all day on Sunday after morning prayers and Church.

I started at Queen Margaret's in September of 1968 at age eleven years old. That first year was one of the most shockingly painful and sad experiences of my life. I had to say goodbye to Mum at home and I left, clutching a stuffed bear she had given for comfort. I was driven by the chauffeur and dropped off by MM to be with hundreds of completely strange people, all girls and women, except the pastor and the tennis and music coaches. First, the matron confiscated all the food items that Beth, MM's cook, had prepared for me, saying that I would be given it at tea times, but I am sorry to say she lied as the only time I ever saw any of it was when a few weeks later, some of the girls and I raided the pantry for a midnight feast. There was a tremendous storm that first night, and I could not sleep for crying and finally went into the bathroom and locked the door, intending to climb out of the window high above the cistern. Once up there, I discovered it was painted shut and spent the rest of the night up there crying. I basically cried nightly for the next three months and begged MM over the Christmas holidays to let me stay at home but to no avail, and once back at school, I cried nightly again for another three months. Any child who didn't settle in was not allowed to see their parents and family members on the midterm weekend or day exit outs. Along with one other girl who also had a difficult time settling in, the other girls teased us mercilessly and played mean practical jokes.

Meals were, of course, at regular times, and being late was not an option as with every other activity. I remember the very first supper so clearly. A girl who was very sad did not feel like eating the plate of food that was set before her. The matron announced that anyone who didn't finish the food on their plate would get it served to them at every meal thereafter until she ate it all. That plate of food appeared at three more meals the next day, and the girl, from sheer hunger, finally ate it for supper. The food was not very appealing compared to what I was used to, and much of it was brought in precooked in bulk—lots of white flour bread and desserts, lard, margarine, sugar, and animal foods. And Sunday supper was always a cold salad as the cooks had the day off. The days were broken up by a midmorning snack of very milky sweet coffee or chocolate and biscuits or shortbread and afternoon tea consisting of tea and bread and jam.

Sundays in those days were always a very somber day with more restrictions, and we had to attend a local church service as well as the usual a.m. and p.m. chapel services. During the first holiday break, upon arriving home, I suddenly realized that school was a better and safer psychological alternative. My home and family were both highly complex and challenging.

So the second year at boarding school was easier, and I made a couple of friends and settled down to being there for the next four years. I had found a way to gain popularity through being daredevil and clowning around. Somewhere midterm that year, my younger sister was sent to join me after it was determined she was not doing well at the local convent school at home, devoid of siblings since my brother had also been sent to a boarding school. At first, it caused me to withdraw from her, mainly I think because she reminded me of all that I wanted to escape at home. However, a few days after her arrival, the matron came to me to say that my sister's menses had started, and she was very upset and asking for me. In that moment, I was reminded of how I had gone through that change alone. And my heart opened to her need for my support and comfort, and we became much closer.

As much as I was homesick, I also remember feeling very apprehensive about my mother coming to the school to take us out for the day, which was allowed twice a term in between the holidays. I felt embarrassed about her but didn't fully understand why until a few years later. Psychotherapy would become a support in the far, distant future many years ahead.

Sometime at the start of the second year, I began to experience the acute discomfort of *genital candida*, or thrush as it's called in the United Kingdom. Back then, the long-term effects of the high animal fat and sugar-laden school diet were not ever mentioned as being linked to this condition, and I suffered for a year and a half with terrible itching and soreness, relieved somewhat with the pessaries and creams that only the matron was allowed to administer but which just added to my overall discomfort and stress. Also, twice a week, I was given a warm salt bath and I spent several weeks over the eighteen months in the school sanatorium feeling unwell and miserable and was also given more antibiotics, which of course, further depleted my compromised immune system and intestinal flora. Added to this state of misery was the fact that I was still chronically constipated and rarely had a natural bowel movement, usually having to strain to move my bowels, which usually only produced a small, hard, dark sinking pieces. It was such a vicious cycle, and my nervous system was not happy.

I arrived home after that holiday to experience my first taste of alcohol (consciously, as I had unknowingly had alcohol as an infant). It happened innocently enough during a visit by our local vicar and his family. Their daughter and I were talking in the kitchen, while the grown-ups were having sherry in the sitting room. Ruth dared me to drink some sherry from the bottle that had been left out, so I did and got very tipsy and later, I had a headache and decided it wasn't something I wanted to do again. *Aah*, innocent youth.

Soon after, I learned that my elder sister had been to stay with our father and his son, our half brother D, born to our first stepmother, Marion (Dad and Marion were by then divorced), and their live-in housekeeper, Mo, who would soon become Dad's third wife. I will say here briefly that Marion had apparently tried to kill Dad by pulling a heavy wooden beam over his back during a heated argument. His back was broken, and he was in a wheelchair for a year but had been awarded sole custody of D. That's when Mo came into the picture to care for baby D and help Dad with his daily needs and therapy.

Even though MM didn't really want us to have anything to do with Dad, she finally allowed me to stay with him on two occasions, once with my elder sister and once on my own. It was a very different experience staying with him compared to life at home. Dad said that even though MM had stopped his visiting us, he was able to get regular news because he was good friends with the parents of one of my closer friends at QM school.

I got to know a bit about his life and that he was into carpentry and did some wood sculptures. He also was into politics and was often trying to get elected to local office and political positions. He took me shopping and bought me a very fashionable and grown-up white leather miniskirt with matching bolero vest. He was experimenting with brewing his own spirits, and when friends came over for dinner one night, he allowed me to sample his latest batch of potato-based Brodka, so called because it was decided it tasted like a cross between brandy and vodka. Dad, Mo, and D all left UK to live in Rhodesia mainly because, he said years later, to escape the custody problems. Anyway, apart from seeing him briefly on the day he dropped off my brother M after a day's outing, I would not see my father and his new family again for thirteen years.

My periods stopped for almost the entire following year at school, and I clearly remember telling Mum and then being so embarrassed when she took me to our local doctor, who then prescribed a low-dose contraceptive pill to regulate the monthly cycles. I was on the pill for the next four years.

My sexual energy was strongly awakened at this time, helped along by a new interest in boys. It was a confusing and awkward time. Life at boarding school chugged along. And by the time I was in the fourth year, aged fifteen, I had started smoking and drinking, and with the help of my girlfriend's parents' broad-mindedness, we were able to support this behavior quite easily. They parked their small motorboat at a canal dock conveniently located on one of our permitted Sunday bicycling routes. Every weekend, we were encouraged to get out of the school grounds and take a picnic lunch to a nearby village, so off we went, very happily, to let our hair down in the comfort of the boat. I pierced my ears with the help of one of these friends, Vicky, equipped with a fat needle and an ice cube we had stolen from the kitchen. However, Vicky fainted, leaving me to finish the job!

Afterward, I learned that I had started a new trend, and on their next leave out, a lot of my peers went off to have their ears pierced in York. And while mine healed nicely, several of their piercings became infected and had to be allowed to close up again. I considered myself lucky. On arrival back home for the following holiday break, to my great surprise, MM approved, saying that she thought I looked like a gypsy.

I had been given the choice by my grandmother as to whether or not I would stay on at QM for two more years or instead attend a one-year finishing college, and I chose the latter, exhilarated by the idea that I could be free from boarding school confinement and restrictions at last. The weeks and months leading up to my last day at QM marked an important change in my life and condition. I should say that during that last year, my friends and I had managed to calculate how to obtain special privileges. Mainly, this was done by being especially helpful in all areas of the school curriculum, getting elected to assist teachers in special projects and also by signing up to participate in a local community volunteer program. We were rewarded by being given permission to go into York on extra days, taking the local rural public bus. (We did, however, test the leniency boundaries once by being seen smoking on the bus and had to work extra hard to win back the trust of the headmistress). We also signed up to take extra double-cooking classes on four days of the week and were not required to attend school lunches on those days. The result of this was that we were able, instead, to eat those foods we had chosen to cook in the classes, which mainly consisted of cakes and pastries, both savory and sweet.

So on my last day of school, the kitchen served a local specialty of deep batter-fried fish and chips and mushy peas. I and my friends were tempted in to this lunch and ate with reckless abandon. Afterward, I went upstairs to prepare for the end-of-year prizes and speeches. I used the lavatory, and when I stood up, one of my earrings fell out on the floor toward the back of the loo. And as I bent to retrieve it, some of the lunch came up, but this caused there to be some stuck in my throat. And I found myself pulling in my stomach muscles, which further released the food that had begun to be eliminated. I had a strange, cold feeling that something was not right and from that day on became afraid of food and eating. So began what would be a three-plus-years-long bout of alternating anorexia and bulimia.

Chapter 6

1973–1977: College, Love, and Eating Disorder

That summer holiday, I became more and more afraid of eating solid or heavy foods and mainly stuck to fruit and salads. I remember one time when I was walking up the stairs at Mum's house and my elder sister called up to me from below asking if I had eaten any breakfast to which I replied that I wasn't hungry. She said she was concerned that I hadn't eaten anything, except fruit in many days and said she would cook me an egg, which I declined, and I had an apple instead. Years later, I realized that I was clearly trying so hard to relax.

I had a couple of boyfriends whom I had met at various private parties during the school holidays. At one of these parties, I also met Henrietta, the youngest daughter of some close friends of MM. Henrietta and I began spending a lot of time together, usually at her family stately home about an hour away. During that summer, I fell head over heels in love and lost my virginity to one of her four older brothers, Jeremy. She tried to warn me that he had other girlfriends and it would be upsetting to be involved with him, but it was too late. He said that he wanted to marry me, have children, and would wait until I was eighteen years old. I believed him, and I was happy in a way that I hadn't ever experienced in my short sixteen years of life.

My grandmother decided that I had a natural inclination and talent for cooking and sewing, and I applied and was accepted into the girls-only Eastbourne College of Domestic Economy down in the southwest coastal city of Eastbourne, Sussex. It was a one-year course in *cordon bleu* cooking, dressmaking, and the home arts as they called it—preparation really for us to become eligible housewives.

One thing that was of some comfort in going there was that Henrietta had started at an exclusive all-girls finishing school to acquire A levels that was close by, and we would meet up on weekends. After the weeks of eating practically nothing at home and attending classes that required students taste the sauces that we were learning to prepare, I found myself so ravenous and was tempted to start eating. And that's when the bulimia reared its ugly head and I became caught in the vicious cycle of feeling starved and then so unbelievably full and wretched, finding purging through contracting my stomach muscles and vomiting the only sure relief. What is amazing is that during that year at college, in spite of my condition, I actually was able to learn a lot, picking up information very quickly in the two subjects that interested me most—cooking and sewing— and graduating in the summer of 1974 with an advanced diploma in *cordon bleu* cooking and dressmaking. It was, however, a gloomy time of my life as I struggled to maintain normalcy in my secret world of alternating starvation and binge purging.

It was sometime during that year at college when Henrietta and I had met up for the day that she asked me what was wrong with my mother. It made me feel very embarrassed. I asked her what she meant, and she just said she thought my mother was different, wasn't normal, which began my internal inquiry into that question of her oftentimes strange behavior. It wasn't until many years later that I told anyone of some of the things that had occurred during my childhood years prior to going to boarding school. Eventually, I also learned some painful and terrible things had happened to Mum over the years—including being given, at eighteen, without her consent, an abortion after being impregnated by a local boy and also later on, electroshock treatments at the private nursing home where she was kept after Dad left us all.

At the end of the college year, I took the train to London to stay a few nights with my elder sister and her boyfriend before going back up to Yorkshire for the summer. They went out quite late in the evening and left me in the flat to watch TV. I had a key, went out, bought some of my favorite ginger wine, and proceeded to drink much of the bottle. As the hours passed by, I began to feel desperately lonely and depressed, took a large knife, and locked myself in the bathroom, intending to slit my wrists. However, at about 4:30 a.m., when my sister and her boyfriend returned, I was still sitting on the edge of the bath just holding the knife to my wrist and sobbing. She begged me to open the door and managed to comfort me, even though she was obviously upset by the event. Strangely enough, we never spoke of it again.

Chapter 7

Working Girl

My grandmother, not wanting me to waste time in the holidays, managed through a connection to get me a job at the local Marks and Spencer clothing factory. I had to get up at 6:00 a.m. in order to catch the bus to town, where another bus left to deliver some twenty other women to the factory. I lasted two weeks there, as the monotony of drawing around a stencil every day began to drive me crazy. After giving my notice at the end of the first week, I was put on the floor, which I enjoyed much more, as I was constantly moved around and given a variety of different tasks. Even sweeping the floor was better than doing the same thing in one position for eight hours a day seven days a week.

The rest of that summer was spent in a fairly depressed state, except for the time I spent staying with Henrietta and seeing Jeremy. However, the bulimia and anorexia for the most part kept me subdued and introverted.

In October of 1974, it was decided that I would spend three months *en famille* with a family in a village near Annecy on the southeast border of France and Switzerland in order to better speak the language, which the French lessons in boarding school had failed to achieve. It was a nerve-racking time once again being in a new and unfamiliar place, my condition was deepening to a new low, and I found myself craving rich foods. I actually stole some Swiss Emmentaler cheese from a supermarket a couple of times and also the cream off the top of the fresh, unpasteurized milk that was delivered to the family with whom I was staying. When Madame F found the cream missing, she was kind but assured me that it wasn't to happen again as it diluted the milk for the rest of the family. I was so humiliated at being discovered and assured her it wouldn't happen again, pleading innocence at having scooped off the best part of the milk, which my body was craving. I wasn't allowed to speak English (the family hardly spoke a word anyway) for the first two months and attended the local college English classes. In the third month, I was introduced to an American girl and we began to meet for coffee in town. I arrived back in Yorkshire in time for Christmas, struggling to remember English words and dreaming in French for several months afterward.

I went for a cooking job interview in January and two weeks later, traveled down to south Devonshire to begin a live-in position as second chef for an à la carte restaurant in the Combe House Hotel where it was run. My eating disorder was greatly enhanced by the overly rich dishes that I was required to cook, and I pampered my cravings for everything rich and creamy using the bulimic purging technique to keep myself empty. I somehow managed to function creatively in my job and in fact, mostly really enjoyed the 1.5 years that I was there. The owners were a lovely, young, Scottish-born couple, Robert and Terri, with three beautiful sons. And being the youngest and probably the most obviously sensitive employee there, they took me under their wing, so to speak. I had one physical mishap, which occurred when I was relighting a gas-powered bain-marie that had blown out. Having waited, as instructed, for fifteen minutes to allow the gas to dissipate, I confidently put the lighter toward the back of the oven and a huge explosion pushed me off the ground backward into the sink unit behind. Terri was mortified, and after first grabbing some ice to place on my hands and face, she rushed me off to the local hospital where they applied some miracle spray solution on my hands that had second-degree burns. My face was not badly affected, but I had no eyelashes, eyebrows, and the front of my hair was singed short. I was kept in the hospital overnight and afterward was off cooking duty for a few days and pampered royally by all.

In those days, I was beginning to happily accept any alcoholic drinks that were offered at the end of my long nightly shifts in the kitchen and remember once being so out of it that I wet my bed in the night, which was most unpleasant. I also took my first driving lessons there in an old Rover that belonged to a local private driving instructor who was friends of the owners. My coordination in those days was poor, and owing to my nervousness and erratic blood sugar swings from the eating disorder, I was not an ideal student. After I left the hotel, I did not resume driving lessons until several years later. I kept in touch with Robert and Terri and even visited them once in my thirties to discover that their youngest son had drowned in a nearby flooded river road over which they were driving after torrential rains had hit the area. They eventually divorced after struggling to come to terms with this tragic event.

I had my eighteenth birthday that June 1975, and during this time, my grandmother arranged for me to follow the family social practice of becoming a debutante and coming out. This involved having a photo and biography posted in *The Tatler* magazine and traveling up to London a few times to attend debutante classes, which involved learning how to walk with a book on my head and how to turn and curtsey in preparation for the royal presentation, debutante ball, and all the possible parties to which I would be invited and obliged to attend. This was all part of the right and done way to meet my future husband. All went according to plan, except that I had eyes only for Jeremy. (And he had eyes for many others.) I went to a few cocktail parties but so often felt that I didn't really fit in. I was nervous and often used alcohol to help me through the evenings' events. I began being courted by the eldest son of the friends of my aunt and uncle. David was quite gentlemanly and fun and once took me to the Royal Opera House in Covent Garden to see Wagner's *Das Valkyries*. My grandmother lent me a fur coat, and I bought a long, sparkly evening gown and borrowed high-heeled shoes from Henrietta. (We were always lending each other clothes.) The opera itself was exhausting, but it was a great experience to go to this famous opera house all dressed up.

When I left Devon, it was decided that I would rent a room in the house of Henrietta's third eldest brother in Northwest London. I got a job as one of several cooks at a gentleman's luncheon club in the city and through word of mouth, started catering for small, private parties. I also spent a few weekends and weeks cooking for my great-aunt and uncle who lived in the southeast county of Kent.

Chapter 8

New Boyfriend

One evening in the autumn, after David ended our yearlong on-and-off relationship, Henrietta insisted that I go with her to have a drink with her boyfriend and meet up with her youngest brother and his musician band members. I was introduced to them all, and one of them—an American, Ben, who shared my taxi home—ended up staying the night and asked me to marry him immediately. I didn't take him seriously and sent him home the next day, but he was not to be deterred and he moved in with me three days later. At twenty-eight, he was ten years older than me, and I suppose I felt safe to be myself and let my hair down with him. And we had a lot fun together. It took several months before I realized he was serious about wanting to marry me, but I was young and very insecure and just laughed it off when he spoke about wanting to be with me forever and have children. The bulimia was just part of my life, and in those days, I easily ate, then purged and just kept my blood sugar topped off with alcohol, cheese, fruit, and sweets.

Later on in that summer of 1976, I accepted a job as an *au pair* to the two young sons of a family in Nice, Southern France. It seemed an exciting adventure, but as I stepped off the airplane, I realized I was very nervous. And that night in the safety of my own apartment, I drank half a bottle of neat vodka, which almost killed me. I pretended I had the flu for the two days after in order to recover, and it left me nervously craving more and more alcohol.

Even though I was always sober when caring for the boys, as soon as I had free time, I went shopping for cheap local beer and wine. I had a couple of flings while I was there but stayed in touch with Ben and afterward, returned to London and we more or less picked where we had left off. I had by now met his parents, who were preparing to sell the family ship-brokering business and the Kensington home they had lived in for the past twenty-five years and return to the United States of America to settle into retirement on the west coast of Florida. Ben and I planned to take a trip the following summer to visit them and travel around the Eastern United States, visiting family and friends in Vermont and Long Island.

That winter, I continued to do freelance cooking and private parties. I remember once getting back very late from catering to a private dinner party and I had drunk a fair amount of my favorite drink, Crabbies Green Ginger Wine. I got into a hot bath and must have passed out because the next thing I knew, it was 8:00 a.m. and I was lying in a bath of very cold water on the verge of suffering severe hypothermia. It was a bit of a wake-up call, but as alcohol was my main source of food that I actually kept down and which didn't make me feel the need to purge, I was still very dependent on it to keep my blood sugar happy and consumed a stable quantity nightly, usually after work when I would meet up with Ben. My food eating disorder was still my darkest secret as yet untold to anyone.

Chapter 9

1977: Attempted Suicide

The eating disorder was beginning to take a toll on my already-fragile emotions, and I had reached a point when I felt desperate and completely alone as if the world were closing in on me. Everything seemed so dark and hopeless, and one morning when everyone had left the house, I calmly went to the bedside, counted out the thirteen Valium pills that were in the prescription bottle that Ben took for his post-broken-neck headaches, and swallowed them all. I wrote a note to him apologizing for my behavior and then lay down on my bed as I began to feel more relaxed, sleepy, and somehow relieved that I no longer had to struggle to be alive.

But as I felt myself slipping away into a strange, unfamiliar sleep, something deep within me knew I didn't really want to die yet. Eventually, I dragged myself along on hands and knees to the lavatory and used my bulimic tricks of pulling in my stomach and purging. Ben returned, found me a few hours later, read the note, and immediately took me to the nearest hospital. After checking my vital signs and learning that I had partially purged the pills, they determined that I didn't need to have my stomach pumped. They brought in a senior nurse to chat with me privately. The hospital nurse knew immediately that I had an eating disorder due to my discolored teeth and thinning hair. That was the first time I had ever heard of the word bulimia. She told me to confide in my boyfriend and to stop taking the pill, which I'd been on since age fourteen to regulate my periods. She also said that I was probably going to be safe from getting pregnant for a couple of weeks but that I should decide on a different form of contraception. That night, I told Ben about my three-year secret, which was such a huge relief. He suggested that we take a holiday and he would try and arrange with his father to get us a passage on a freight ship to America and then we made passionate love.

Chapter 10

1977–1978: First Trip to the United States on a Ship and Pregnancy

Several weeks later, we were traveling to Amsterdam, Holland, to await sailing orders and passage on the forty-four-thousand-ton Yugoslavian grain freight ship that was going over to New Orleans in ballast. We spent another two weeks in Holland before we actually sailed from Rotterdam harbor on May 28. I remember feeling very free. No doubt the easy access to hemp in Holland helped, but it was partly due to the fact that I hadn't had a bulimic episode since the suicide attempt and I was enjoying, with some caution, eating without discomfort or fear or remorse.

For the entire voyage, I suffered, or so I thought, from seasickness but generally, only in the mornings. The crew of eleven men spoke only Russian and Yugoslavian with only the captain and the boson speaking a little broken English. It mattered little, for they treated us like royalty, showering us with free duty-free gifts. And the cook allowed me to make Ben a birthday cake, and he then made one for me as our birthdays are two days apart, complete with half-egg-shell candles filled with alcohol that was lit. I remember feeling quite certain that I did not wish to eat any meat at that time and requested fish instead to which the cook kindly complied. However, the only fish they had, surprisingly, was calamari. And it was cooked in the same way every day, namely deep-fried, which was, I have to say, acceptably tempting and tasty.

I was aware of the small swimming pool, which obviously hadn't been used in years and asked the captain if it could be easily cleaned and filled to which he assented and so it was that we found ourselves helping to clean and fill the pool. Once finished, a red tape was stretched across it and I, as the only woman on board, was given the honor of cutting it with everyone gathered around. And then the crew all jumped in with their clothes on and they handed out wine and food and played music all night. I drank only a half cup of the wine because it tasted strange. My taste buds were accurate, for in the morning, I had a splitting headache as did all the crew. It turned out that the wine was reconstituted from concentrate and had not been properly diluted—lethal stuff plus all the sulfites.

I spent much of the trip up at the bow, reading and watching with great pleasure and contentment the dolphins that swam with us and the vast expanse of sea as it stretched out in front of the massive bulk of steel that was our home for those two weeks. It was a magical time.

We docked up the Mississippi River, just outside New Orleans, on Saturday, June 11. And the customs tugboat took us from the ship to the US customs and immigration hut where our passports were stamped. We took a taxi to the French Quarter, found an inexpensive motel, and shared a wonderful dinner of whole crab and a pitcher of cold beer. Afterward, we wandered the streets, listening to a variety of great jazz musicians serenading the balmy Southern city. It was a rich and special experience before we flew on to Florida to where Ben's parents had settled in retirement.

Ben's parents asked us to house-sit for three weeks, and as we had basically spent all our savings in Holland and were too shy to ask for help, we ended up buying some bait in order to catch fish off their dock. We happily ate the flounder and catfish we caught for those few weeks! I remember on several occasions while we were there experiencing a fluttering in my abdomen as though I had a trapped muscle. I would massage my tummy until it stopped but didn't think too much about it. After his parents returned, we answered an ad to deliver a pickup truck to a place in Vermont in order that we could visit Ben's aunt and uncle there. That was a very lovely week staying on their farm in the Airstream trailer they used for winter trips to Mexico. Then we went down to Long Island to stay with Ben's college friend Bob and his lady, Lois, and we all literally lived on the beach for the next six weeks. I had a part-time job, opening clams and making soup at a popular roadside clam bar. It seemed my eating disorder had almost vanished apart from the occasional bulimic moments when I got stressed, and I was filling out nicely, especially in my cheeks and breasts.

After having spent almost three months in the United States of America, we flew back home to London. Upon arrival, Henrietta took one look at me and said, "You are pregnant!" Even though I was twenty years old, I was extremely naive and I was not at all in touch with the workings of my own body. I did not really believe I was pregnant because I did not feel pregnant, but she made me an appointment to see a local doctor who diagnosed a bladder and uterine infection. He prescribed antibiotics, which I didn't take because Henrietta insisted I was pregnant and immediately took me to the nearest clinic to be properly diagnosed. And within minutes, the pregnancy was confirmed, even though it hardly showed in my stomach. They estimated that I was almost four months along. In that moment, I found myself in what I now describe as my first experience of being in a state of grace.

The news filled me with contentment, and I became so completely relaxed that I stopped being bulimic instantly. I felt so happy in this newfound knowledge and condition and started enjoying food and eating in a way that I had never known before, simply allowing myself to eat whatever my body wanted. I was guided to delicious-tasting food with a vegetarian slant—like bean-and-cheese burritos; milkshakes; and delicious, fresh croissants, cakes, and pastries from the local French bakery. One favorite was a vanilla gateaux that had a layer of almond marzipan and real whipped cream in the middle, almond marzipan all around the sides and on top another layer of whipped cream that was then topped with fresh strawberries and kiwi fruit. I was blissfully happy all throughout the pregnancy.

The only moment of stress came when I telephoned Yorkshire and told my grandmother that I was pregnant. She was furious and insisted that I should go home immediately so that she and Mum could help raise the baby, as she felt I was too young and not capable. When I said no and that it would probably bring on a miscarriage, she replied that that would be the best thing for everyone. I am sorry to say that I abruptly hung up on her and we didn't speak for several weeks afterward. Mum was none too happy either but was more worried and gentle with me. As I said, Ben had been wanting to marry me ever since we had met and I now accepted his new proposal. We had a civil marriage in late October and a party afterward put on by the dear friends with whom we lived. Mum came to the wedding dressed in dark gray and black and looked like she was at funeral. MM did not come, but we reconciled once she had accepted that I was now married (shotgun weddings were not in her repertoire). We went up to Yorkshire for Christmas that year, and from then on, there was much more support and acceptance. She even had a beautiful new pram sent to our London flat.

Chapter 11

Birth of a Beautiful, Healthy Daughter

I attended pregnancy/birthing classes and was hoping to have as natural a birth as possible, though chose to be in the local hospital, which was very supportive to mothers wishing to have the least amount of interference in the birthing process unless absolutely necessary. I went into labor on January 14, 1978, after washing all the downstairs windows, and miraculously, my daughter was born beautiful and healthy after sixteen hours of intense labor pain and tearing. As they stitched me up, they lay the baby in a crib next to me and she appeared to be looking straight at me. And I heard a voice say that she would be my greatest teacher, and I just knew it was the truth. Because of her presence, my whole life turned around.

I was determined to be a good mother to give my daughter the best I could and certainly not duplicate what I had been given—such naivete.

It seems that I had subconsciously traded the anorexic/bulimic phase for a bowel-movement obsession, as I was still often constipated and usually wouldn't leave the house before I could move my bowels and that was usually aided by a cup of English black tea and milk and a few puffs of a cigarette taken quietly alone. When my daughter was just a couple of weeks old, I opened the *Teach Yourself Yoga* book, which had been given to me by a friend and former alcoholic that had found her recovery this way. She had told me that AA only swapped sugar for alcohol, opening my eyes for the first time to the effects of sugar, which was a revelation for me.

So two weeks after the birth, I began to learn some basic hatha yoga and immediately noticed some wonderful positive changes so much so that I have practiced it almost daily for the past forty-three years, except when I was on my days of the month. I started to hold myself differently, learned to breathe more deeply, and generally felt more confident and calm.

I then began to be attracted to wholegrain bread, grains, and beans to supplement my still-fairly dairy-and-animal-food-rich diet. One dish that I prepared with some frequency was traditional-style cassoulet, which I made in the large, orange, oval Le Creuset enameled pot (which I still have and use) that had been given as a wedding present. The recipe, which is still in my head, consists of previously soaked navy beans, onions, garlic, tomatoes, and kielbasa sausages cooked for about two through three hours and served with fresh French baguettes. The aroma, taste, and texture was deeply satisfying on many levels. This was my introduction to the delicious, rich bean dishes that I would come to rely on in years to come.

We traveled up to Yorkshire for the christening of our beautiful baby daughter when she was two and a half months old. She was dressed in the silk-and-lace christening robes and bonnet that had been made for my great-grandmother back in the 1800s, and it was a beautiful service held in the ancient chapel up in the dales moors region of North Yorkshire. We named her Rose.

It snowed heavily the next day, and we were snowed in and unable to go back to the London flat for two weeks. Once we got back, I was challenged by the onset of double mastitis and infection and had to abandon breastfeeding her. The following morning, I awoke to a splitting migraine headache that would be with me almost constantly for the next two years but which was really another incentive and catalyst that prompted me toward great changes in my diet and lifestyle. The baby was very stressed for several days, not wanting any substitute for mother's milk. And eventually, I sought the advice of a nursery nurse, who straight away calmed me down and immediately gave my poor, darling, dehydrated baby some water followed by a bottle of the latest so-called healthy soy milk substitute formula. And she began to take the bottle and thrive again. Those early months of motherhood were such a mixed blessing. I was so high being mother to this beautiful, precious child, who took my breath away every day.

But I had sleepless nights and painful days with the migraine headaches, which caused me to be feeling tired and stressed on a regular basis. A dear friend was moving to the United States of America and offered to sublet her flat to us, so we moved across the road to the first flat of our own, which felt wonderful after years of shared digs. Our lovely neighbor, Mrs. Grovenburg, insisted that she take baby for a few hours here and there so I could either have a long nap or go and do some shopping or even allow Ben and I to go out for a drink to relax.

I found it extremely hard to let baby out of my sight for even a second but gradually managed to gratefully and sensibly accept her offers. And Mrs. Grovenburg had suggested that I have a little beer or Guinness a few times a week to fortify me as I had lost some weight rather quickly when the migraines started due to lost appetite. I was introduced to a wonderful place to shop called Neals Yard, which in those days, sold bulk grains, beans, flours, and natural skin and hair products. I started eating plain roasted peanut and almond butters and drinking chamomile tea to help sleep and echinacea to help the migraines. These were all revelations in my initiation into the world of applying natural alternative food and medicine.

The first thing I did to try and cure the migraines was to have a general checkup and then a brain scan and all that was determined was that I had blocked sinuses. After many weeks, a friend suggested I go to an Indian acupuncturist and that had an incredible effect. As soon as Mrs. Naidoo put in the needles, the migraine went away, but as soon as she removed them, it came back. She did some bloodletting between the third-eye region and suggested that I stop eating cheese, sugar, and chocolate, which I did but with little effect to the migraines, which were relentless.

I started making children's hand-smocked dresses and potpourri from the roses in the garden and sold my art at the Swiss Cottage and Covent Garden weekend markets.

We took a trip to Florida to stay with Ben's parents in their new place of retirement and on returning, decided we would move to the United States of America the following year. Just prior to leaving United Kingdom, I met up with a friend in London and noticed her beautiful handmade Mary Poppins-style carpetbag that pleased me very much. I had a strong intuition that these bags would sell really well in the United States and decided that I would start a business distributing them in Florida. I contacted Harry Hart and Loretta Quartey, an English couple who owned the company Carpet Bags, and they invited me and my daughter to go and visit them in Norfolk, which we did for a weekend trip. They told us that they had been appalled at the barren, desertlike state in many countries because of the over farming of trees, which they saw on various filming trips to Africa. They decided to raise money to help third-world countries reclaim the desert and founded a charity called Green Deserts. They bought up secondhand, natural wool and cotton carpets and antique rugs to make their bags. Then they were carefully washed with pure soap, dried, then cut and fashioned into beautiful practical bags of all sizes and shapes. It is still a thriving business in England.

I needed money that we didn't have to start my business, but neither my parents nor Ben's were willing to help us, so I put the idea on hold. They also were my first exposure to the idea of macrobiotics, having been practicing this way of life since the late sixties, but it wasn't until a few years later that I was ready to really take notice of what they were trying to share with me in their gentle, nonintrusive way.

Chapter 12

Beginning New Life in America

So in December 1979, we moved to the United States to be near Ben's parents in Florida and to start a new life. Initially, we stayed with them until we found a place to rent in the New Year.

I was happy to be warm after a lifetime of cold and damp weather in England, but it was hard adjusting to some of the American ways, and for a couple of years, I was quite homesick for England. We traveled back to visit family and friends the following spring, and it was only then that I realized that my life in the United States was actually helping me to see some things in a different light. My English roots were my platform from which I had chosen to leave to explore an alternative way of life, and I began to open up further to some new ideas. We rented a big, old Spanish-style house near the Ringling Art School, and my brother came from England to join us.

The migraines were still happening daily and sometimes so badly I had to stay in the bedroom with the curtains closed for a couple of days. The friend who had introduced me to yoga suggested that I go to see a naturopath/chiropractor who had helped her through a difficult health-related time. I got an appointment immediately and over the next three months, worked closely with him (I wish I could remember his name) as he systematically eliminated foods that might be triggers, put me on a custom-made regimen of several supplements, and gave various chiropractic treatments at each visit. Toward the end of the third month, he sent me home on a Friday, toting a three-day supply of extra-strong supplements and forewarned me that I was probably going to suffer the worst migraines of my life over the coming days and on the third day, would wake up migraine free. And that was exactly what happened!

And now, forty years later, I have not had a single other migraine and I thank that man wholeheartedly for making such a big difference to my life and well-being as it surely was a large part of my journey toward overall better health and healthier ways of taking care of myself.

In this new migraine-free state, I began to make more interesting vegetarian-style dishes, though still including dairy, especially butter and English-style cheeses like Wensleydale and Stilton, which I brought over whenever I returned from a trip there.

I think the glorious west coast Florida climate was instrumental in helping in my new attraction to a healthier way of eating and living, and I started to explore the Edgar Cayce dietary guidelines for detoxifying. I also began to replace all the commercially made household cleaning and personal care products for natural ones. Edgar introduced the idea that all the chemicals, preservatives, and artificial scents used in those commercial brands were very toxic to the human system. This was indeed a great revelation.

Chapter 13

Separation and New Business Venture

After a temporary preschool teaching job I had secured ended, Ben and I were juggling stuffing envelopes for a direct marketing company and selling Amway products. One day, I discovered an interesting clothing shop in town owned by wonderful woman called Anita who was making most of the items herself. I made up a few dresses to show her that she took on as consignments, and they sold quickly.

We had to move after a year and found a sweet, Spanish-style house in the artistic area of downtown Sarasota. But our marriage was not going so well, and Ben and I separated for the first time. And he went up to find work in New York. Anita and I joined as partners and with the landlords' permission, converted my garage into a sewing studio for our business venture, Fourth World. We designed and made beautiful clothing out of suede and leather, and our mutual attraction to vintage fabrics, buttons, and trims resulted in some very artistic and pleasing creations. We took custom orders and on one occasion, made a costume for the woman who trained the Ringling brothers circus clowns on their graduation night gala. Another costume we made was a pelican outfit for a woman who delivered singing telegrams. I made several items of clothing for family and friends, including the wedding dress for my younger sister's wedding.

I really enjoyed my initial freedom as a single mother, happy to be on my own for the first time in my life. I took a six-week yoga course given by the people whose book I had used to teach myself and added meditation to my repertoire, which I seemed to naturally be able to practice and which added an extra level of feeling to my newly found inner peace and calm.

I remember in those days waking up with such joy and excitement about my life, and the new business was a great deal of fun, even though we didn't make much money. Anita and her boyfriend introduced me to an interesting new life of work and play. I felt as though I was being able to catch up / have some of the fun that I missed out on in my late teens because of the eating disorder and by having a child so young. She was also the first person who had ever suggested that eating slowly was very beneficial, even though at the time, I didn't get it at all, and she also introduced me to controlled fasting and high colonic cleanses recommended by Dr. Christopher Hills. I was utterly amazed at what had accumulated and been stored in my body and after the first couple of rounds, experienced for the first time in my life, a healthy, well-formed, normal bowel movement.

During one of these fasting programs, which usually lasted for about three weeks, and when Rose was with her grandparents for the weekend, I rode my bike to the beach and lay down in the sun, intending to just relax and take in a little sun and swimming. As I was lying there, I decided to do some conscious breathing and meditation as I had learned to do in my yoga classes, and after what seemed like just a few minutes, I suddenly became aware that my body was slowly rising up off the sand. Even though I was in a deeply calm meditative place, I wanted to confirm that what I was experiencing really was happening and not just a dream thought. So I simply raised my right hand with flat palm and very slowly and carefully, as I wished not to break the moment, moved it toward my torso and it went unobstructed under my levitated body. I slowly drew my hand back to my side and remained in that state for again what seemed like a few more minutes. I just felt very happy and grateful to have experienced this. When I came down, I looked at my watch and one hour had passed by. This special experience was the first of what has turned out to be a variety of many others since—all unique and different but somehow reminding me of how important it is for my spirit to be nourished and given support in order that it can live freely.

As the controlled fasting continued and the months passed by, I began to understand an underlying cause of my lifelong struggle with constipation and that I had most likely not ever eliminated the fetal waste and was clogged up from birth. I also realized that my way of thinking was changing, and I saw that I had been living a rather self-ish life with a narrow vision and view of the world. In the last year in Florida, I was introduced to and experienced the euphoric effects of cocaine and freshly harvested hallucinogenic mushrooms. I continued to experiment with fasting and colonics, the process of washing out of the colon, until I ended the last fasting period I ever did by taking cocaine, which played a number on my new, more sensitive condition of health.

In January 1985, Ben and I had a reconciliation and I felt it was time to leave Florida. So he flew down from New York, and we rented a U-Haul and drove north together.

I immediately started craving more cooked and warming food in the frigid winter of the Northeast while I still continued to experiment with various alternative healing and cleansing modes, including wheat grass juice, apple cider vinegar, and maple syrup with cayenne and fresh carrot juice. Ben and I played with cocaine for that first year in New York, and I had started drinking coffee until my nervous system and adrenals couldn't handle it anymore. I stopped both coffee and cocaine almost overnight, preferring after all the high of being clean and sober.

Introduction to Macrobiotics, Enlightenment, and the Art of Chewing

Chapter 14

The Art of Chewing

In the early spring of 1986 while living in a sixth-floor walk-up apartment in New York City, a little paperback book arrived in the post, a gift sent from some friends in England with whom I had stayed a few months earlier.

Within hours after reading the book, I was seated with a small bowl of freshly cooked brown rice and chopsticks and started to follow the author's suggestion to begin eating, for the first time in my twenty-nine years of life, consciously. What I experienced during the next two hours of silent, purposeful, counted chewing was so extraordinary that it changed and has shaped my life ever since.

In October 1985, I returned to the United Kingdom with Rose to visit family and also stayed once again with my carpetbag friends in Norfolk, purposefully to make a hand-chosen order of carpetbags to take back to the States to stimulate some new interest and hoped-for sales. I was invited to become officially the East Coast United States of America representative salesperson for Carpet Bags Inc., which I happily accepted. During this visit, Harry and Loretta spoke more in depth about the macrobiotic lifestyle that they had been embracing for the past twenty years and offered me miso soup; adzuki beans with kombu and winter squash; fresh kale (both had been harvested from their garden); and pressure-cooked, short-grain brown rice for supper. I had never eaten any of these foods before, still preferring the fruits, nuts, seeds, and snacks that I had come to enjoy since living in Florida. I also wasn't very good at chewing (even though Anita had highly recommended it) and actually had probably never really chewed anything ever, so at the time, I really wasn't so much impressed by this food. What did impress me, though, was the energy of Loretta and Harry—their awareness; calm confidence; humility; empathy; compassion; generosity; and open-hearted, expanded vision of so much. They were so easygoing, and they weren't trying to impress or change me, just confident in what they were sharing because they had been practicing and living this way of life for so many years. Nonetheless, they impressed me deeply.

Something clicked for me on that visit, and I knew this was what I wanted for me, my life, and my family. It piqued my interest like a child digging in the garden and finding a buried treasure. Even though I knew very little about which they spoke, I was lit up, turned on, realized that I had found something very special and wonderful, and felt extraordinarily excited with some apprehension as to all the possible changes that I sensed would come about in the not-too-distant future. I voiced my keen interest in wishing to know more, and Harry and Loretta said that they would order a copy of George Ohsawa's little book on the macrobiotic diet, which was currently out of stock, and have it sent to me in New York.

During that visit with Harry and Loretta, I also learned that one of their Green Deserts re-desertification projects had been launched in Southern Spain and was being run as a work/exchange holiday program. They invited us to go there the following year, and I offered my services to cook for everyone as our work barter, which was happily accepted. And it was agreed that we would try and arrange to go to Almeria, Spain, the following year for two weeks.

After spending some more time with my family in Yorkshire, we flew back to New York. And I decided that I really needed to live out of the city in the countryside, and we began to travel upstate at the weekends in an effort to find an affordable place to either buy or rent.

I also became pregnant during this time but felt very ill and that there was something not right with the baby. I terminated the pregnancy, asking forgiveness to my unborn child. Almost immediately, I felt well again.

Over the next few months, I made calls to several high-end shops like Henri Bendel, Bergdorf Goodman, Macy's, and some small specialty boutique shops in the village. My intuition for the timing seemed to be on target, for they all placed substantial orders for both the newer tapestry-style bags and the all-wool-and-cotton antique carpetbags. I also signed up to have a stall at a couple of the big street fairs. It was a very good season and year for Carpet Bags.

The little macrobiotic book that Harry and Loretta promised to send arrived a few weeks later. After reading it, I was very curious and excited to try George Ohsawa's suggestions that one could achieve spiritual enlightenment by eating very simply and chewing everything, including liquids, very well. Without fully understanding what he meant by this state of being but sensing it was something great, I decided to follow his remedy to help irregular menstruation as I had not yet had a period since the pregnancy termination. This included eating cooked short-grain brown rice eaten with a roasted sesame seed and sea salt condiment called gomashio and drinking a special, blended Japanese herb tea called MU number sixteen exclusively for five days in a row.

So I straight away went to the health food shop, bought all the ingredients, cooked some short-grain brown rice on which I sprinkled a little of the shop-bought gomashio, boiled up some of the tea, and then sat down to begin my first macrobiotic lesson in chewing food—counting, at Mr. Ohsawa's suggestion, every mouthful one hundred times. Using chopsticks for the first time, I picked up some of the rice, put it in my mouth, and began to chew and count, "One. Two. Three. Four. Five. Six. Seven." And as I was counting, my eyes closed and it seemed that all sounds around me had vanished. After barely finishing the first mouthful, I began to have a most wonderful and extraordinary experience. It seemed that a tremendous heat was being generated inside and around me and that a portal was opening on the top of my head through which golden light began pouring into my body and streaming and circulating throughout every part—beginning through my head and shoulders and then down my back, arms, and legs and out of my hands, fingers, feet, and toes. As I continued chewing and counting to one hundred, I began to hear the most beautiful music I have ever heard that was then followed by angelic voices singing so very sweetly. And then it seemed that I was being channeled to receive vital information about my family's condition, world events, and general universal information. I was in what I now call a state of grace and bliss, and I was hooked.

For the next five days as I continued to eat the rice in this manner, I walked on air with sunlight coursing through my veins and entire being.

On the third day, I began menstruating and I was convinced that I had stumbled on some magical formula for optimal life of great health and enjoyed the best flow period that I had ever had. However, that was to be the last time I would menstruate for eight years. I also became very unsure about food but more and more sure about chewing and the wonderful sense of well-being and calm that this simple act manifested in me.

We had been taking weekend trips upstate to the New Paltz and Woodstock areas of Ulster County, New York, to try and find a place to either buy or rent. And after a couple of false starts, we ended up renting a lovely old farmhouse called Shellbark Farm near the village of Accord. We rented a U-Haul van, and on a lovely, sunny spring morning, Rose and I drove up there to begin our interesting, new country life. Ben remained working in New York City and came up on weekends, and I straight away got involved in the community. I joined the local High Falls Food Co-op as a working member and would take Rose there once a week to help bag up the bulk items. We most often ended bagging the raisins, which others tended to avoid because of the stickiness but delighted Rose who loved to snack on them. We met a lovely Russian woman called Mourka and her two children at the High Falls Co-op semiannual party, and we instantly became lifelong friends. Life in the countryside suited me well, and my inclination to be surrounded in and by all things natural was supported more readily. I discovered the pleasure of various essential oils and enjoyed having an abundance of big, beautiful plants inside my home. I began to be more aware of the fact that city living is very noise polluting. The sweet silence living without any other houses, people, or machines close by was exhilarating. I started a vegetable garden and walked around the horse pasture, collecting horse manure for the sweet corn, peas, and cucumbers that I planted. My newfound interest in a macrobiotic diet led me to start making some interesting, new food dishes albeit without any real understanding of balance or the consideration of my deep-rooted birth condition. I taught myself how to make amazake, natto, seitan, tofu, and sweet-rice pounded mochi. I dried, hand shelled, and roasted the seeds from the winter squash and sunflowers I had grown.

Friends and relatives came to stay, and I remember that I rarely actually ate anything with them anymore as it became impossible to talk and eat at the same time. When they left, then I could relax to eat silently, carefully chewing everything until it was liquid. This practice was one of, if not, the greatest practical personal gift I had been given in my life so far, even though I had no understanding of how far off I was in creating healthy, balanced meals. I was working from an intellectual place and simply following recipes in the macrobiotic books that eventually would be revealed as much too salty, dry, and contracting for my condition and best health.

Chapter 15

Travels

That summer, Rose and I traveled back to England, then went over to Spain and had a wonderful experience staying in a deserted village near Los Molinos del Rio de Aguas in Almeria Province. Over the past decades, hundreds of villagers have just packed a suitcase and headed for the cities to start new, hopefully more prosperous, easier, urban lives. They left behind their beautiful, handmade homes, furniture, and clay pots and abandoned the carefully tended irrigated hillside terraces, crucial for sustaining vegetal growth and halting the advance of desertification caused by the heavy rains. This departure has dramatically changed the entire eco structure of much of Southern Spain. Without the care, the rains began to wash away any growth, and as the amount of trees and vegetal matter declined, the less carbon dioxide and rain; hence, the arrival of Green Deserts.

It was thrilling to be a part of this vitally important work that Harry and Loretta had initiated. People were invited to do a work-trade holiday, putting in four hours a day in exchange for helping with the various projects. A magnificent outhouse was built/created by a man called Tom, and there was a sign on the entrance that read, "Uncle Tom's Cabin." It consisted of a fifty-gallon, black, plastic, empty olive drum/barrel with a well-made sturdy platform where one stood and squatted over the hole while staring at a view that took your breath away. When the barrels were filled two thirds, they had the lid put back on and sealed and were rolled off to an area away from the buildings to compost for six months before the contents were then spread around the terraces to help build back up the nutrients in the topsoil.

Much work was done on rebuilding the terrace walls and planting the terraces with native shrubs like capers, rue, olive, almond, and fruit trees. I volunteered my time as cook and housekeeper during our stay and was feeding sometimes as many as twelve volunteers at a sitting, all meals cooked on a one-burner stove with a small oven. I made chickpea stews, hummus, polenta, and corn bread, and we had a few fresh vegetables from the newly planted terraced garden beds along with local almonds, fruit, olive oil, olives, and capers.

All the water was carried in to the casa in buckets collected from the irrigation overflow, and that's where every day, we stood to take our rather-chilly showers. In the afternoons, when nearly everyone was having siesta, Rose and I walked into the hills to a magnificent blue lagoon surrounded by flowering oleander and almond trees. Whenever we approached the lagoon, the turtles who were sunbathing on the rocks around the sides would slip quickly into the pool. We would swim and explore the deserted houses in the area and chew on sweet, warm carob pods. I stuffed my knapsack with enough to take back to grind up to make puddings. That trip planted a seed in me that would slowly grow. A quite magical experience altogether.

Two weeks later, we were at the house in Sledmere, Yorkshire, for the rather-grand noble wedding of Henrietta—quite a contrast! We returned to New York afterward, and I immediately signed up to have a stall at the New York Sterling Forest Renaissance Faire to show carpetbags. The fair lasted for seven weekends, and it was a very enjoyable experience.

Chapter 16

My Prison Pen Pal

I had started subscribing to a couple of magazines: One was *Mother Earth*, and the other was the *East West Journal*. In the September 1986 issue of the *East West Journal*, the editors were giving readers an opportunity to donate a gift subscription to their prisoner pen pal program, and I decided to send one in. A few weeks later, I received a letter from Greenville Correctional Facility sent by a prisoner called Delmo, thanking me very much and so began an interesting friendship.

Over the next few years, I shared all that I had come to know about macrobiotics, yoga, meditation, shiatsu, and tai chi. Delmo was hungry for spiritual nourishment and had been studying Zen Buddhism. He started practicing chewing everything he ate very well, and I was able to bring him in any natural foods that were hermetically sealed, like rice cakes, tahini, nut butters, sealed ramen noodles, and soups.

When I first met him, he was carrying a lot of extra weight, and as a 6'2" black man who was working out in the gym daily, he was by all accounts a big presence. The change in his appearance after a few weeks of his newfound practice and regimen was quite dramatic. He lost a lot of weight and started to look quite healthy and vibrant in spite of his incarceration circumstances. He was eventually moved to a local facility and invited Rose and I to attend various family day picnics, including a couple of the Zen family gatherings that the prison held in the summer months.

Chapter 17

Trip to South Africa 1988

I was happy on my macrobiotic diet but didn't have a clue as to what I was doing to my internal organs. I ate grain and grain products almost exclusively. Having newly realized that sugar and dairy were not good for humans, I easily stopped eating them, substituted with grain sweets and vegetable alternatives, and also began to restrict my daughter's intake and intervene in her healthy intuition in a not-so-healthy effort to do right by her. My poor daughter had to go through all these phases with me but trusted me as her mother. Luckily, many of her requests and choices turned out to be much more balancing than my own.

Around this time, I had a strong feeling that I needed to reconnect with my father who was living in South Africa. I had not seen him in thirteen years, and he had obviously never met his firstborn grandchild, then eight years old. It happened to coincide with my half brother's own plans to travel from South Africa to Canada via England, and it was decided that we would meet in London and travel up to Yorkshire all together so that we could all connect properly for the first time in our lives.

At first, my grandmother and mother were outraged that I would suggest such a visit, feeling it was digging up old skeletons and wounds, but they relented and were so very happy to meet David, who was undoubtedly a dear and sweet person and who had also gone through some very traumatic childhood experiences of his own with our Dad.

We parted a few days later, and Rose and I took a twelve-hour flight to Johannesburg, where we were met by my father. I felt instantly relieved to see him after so many years, and the first two weeks were very good. He drove us several hours back to his property on the outskirts of Mafeking in Bophuthatswana, where he had gone to the trouble of converting a small outbuilding into a comfortable studio complete with mini kitchen and gas stove. Sometime during the weeks before our arrival, he had asked if he could stock up on any special foods that we might like and so he had kindly procured sacks of grain, flour, a variety of vegetables, and a large quantity of peanuts in their shells, which are an everyday food item in that part of the world. He then took us to the local health shop, where I found soy milk, tahini, unsweetened jam, peanut butter, and rice cakes. I was able to make my own tofu with the soy milk, using lemon juice instead of nigiri to curdle. I shared my newfound pleasure of chewing and some of the macrobiotic home remedies that I was experimenting with out of the book I had bought called *Macrobiotic Home Remedies*. And for the first time in fifteen years, my father's thrombosis-afflicted leg was not red and swollen and began to heal, and he said he was having the best bowel movements he had ever experienced in his life. On one of the last conversations I ever had with Dad on the telephone, he said he always kept a small jar of brown rice on his desk and periodically would take a small handful and chew it all until it was liquid—one of the remedies I had shared and had used there for Rose and me to help eliminate intestinal worms.

I had been introduced to tai chi martial art form in Yorkshire that summer and would walk out to the edge of the town, a few blocks away to practice tai chi walking in the bush. Almost every day, I would meet a happy group of barefoot children, wearing rags and carrying buckets on their heads, singing sweet songs on their way to get water for the day from the public well. They invited me (and Rose when she had come with me) to meet their grandmother, and we discovered that all five children were being looked after by their grandmother while their parents were hundreds of miles away, earning money to support everyone. They weren't able to go to school because the law at that time excluded any child from going to school if they did not have the required uniform and shoes to wear. Shocking but true. I had enrolled Rose in a local public school and made her a couple of white short-sleeved blouses to comply with the uniform guidelines. She already had suitable skirts and white socks and sandals.

So we went into town and were able to buy all the children Chinese sandals and cotton socks, and Rose went through her suitcase and picked out almost half of her clothes to give to the older girls. We met the children the following day and walked with them home to their grandmother. They were so happy to have the clothes, and we were offered very weak coffee to drink and were told that they all, children included, drank very diluted coffee every day as a homeopathic drink. And the grandmother told us that they only have it strong when they are ill. It seems much of the Western world has it backward.

But things with my father began to unravel, as I started to open up about my childhood without his presence. And he in turn started to drink heavily and became outraged at some of the things I told him, saying I was making it all up and that I should see a shrink because I was obviously out of my mind. I began to shut down but took his offer of seeing a woman psychiatrist who thankfully knew that my father was alcohol dependent and counseled me through the rest of the stay. I changed our tickets, and the three-month stay ended with my father dropping us off at the airport and saying, "Have a nice life," with no hug goodbye. It was a deeply traumatic visit, and when we arrived back in England, I was feeling grateful that he had in fact left us all as young children and with some new understanding and empathy for what my mother and then my half brother had endured living with and growing up with him. However, I will add that we reconciled during the year that my stepmother was dealing with breast cancer. Dad called me in Hawaii to tell the news and asked if I could send a few special health food items to aid in her treatment that weren't available in South Africa. I naturally sent off the items, but sadly, she did not recover. He was sober for a year afterward and sent all five of his children a copied letter asking forgiveness of his behavior. He married wife number four, which did not last. We spoke on and off over the years, and in 2018, the year I had decided to go and visit him again in Africa, he died in his sleep.

Chapter 18

Starved

After spending Christmas holidays in Yorkshire, we returned to New York, and during the first evening there, while standing in the bathroom preparing for bed, Ben told me that I looked like death. I hadn't looked at myself in a mirror naked until then, and I was so deeply shocked at how malnourished I looked. And suddenly, I was very afraid.

The shock of seeing myself seemed to make me lose more weight. I sought the help of several well-respected senior macrobiotic counselors, all of whom had widely differing opinions and suggestions, and it was a very confusing and frightening time. One advised me that I was starving to death and told me to eat anything, but because I had no real ability to make wise choices for myself because I was so malnourished at this point, most foods I either cooked myself or ate in restaurants made me feel sick and nauseous. Very occasionally, when in a calm inner state, I would be guided to healthier things— like the sweet root vegetables dish called nabe, which was amazingly delicious and seemed to be very relaxing. But after an hour, I'd be starving again. Then I would eat something else that would subsequently make me feel tight in my *solar plexus* and heart region. When I was empty, I didn't have pain and tightness.

One person, Rochelle, who had been giving me regular support with shiatsu treatments, invited me to go to a macrobiotic workshop hosted by another senior counselor. I ended up getting a private consultation with this person who diagnosed *candida* and advised me to cut out all fermented food for a year and all sweets, except grapefruit. I went home feeling hopeful and wanting to believe yet unsure. I had come to enjoy miso soup, sourdough bread, tempeh, homemade amazake, and natto and understood that they were an important part in the macrobiotic diet. It would be some time before I realized that I just did not know how to best prepare these beneficially supporting foods.

On one occasion, I had dreamt of eating clams, and when I told the counselor, he recommended clam juice. It was so salty, and I got even tighter from it. I was chronically hungry and uncomfortable in my body.

Then one day, after another phone conversation, he said that he couldn't help me anymore and that I needed to see a psychiatrist. Soon after, I became bulimic again and struggled on my own for several more months. Rochelle, now realizing the severity of my condition, strongly suggested that another senior macrobiotic counselor, an American called Denny Waxman, could likely help me. But when I finally got the courage to call him, I was too arrogant to seek his help, offering instead that I had something valuable to share with him about my experience with bulimia and anorexia. As I became more undernourished and tight, strangely enough, my spirit became very strong. I didn't have much to buffer or block experiences, could foresee things before they manifested, and had a knowing sense of what would happen as a result of a previous action. I was frightened and awestruck at the same time and caught in the vicious cycle, nearly always hungry and steadily losing more weight.

Chapter 19

Dying?

There is no force on Earth more powerful than the will to live.
—James Franco

In April of 1989, I had a strong premonition that if I stayed where I was that I would surely die, and the idea that my precious child would find me dead one morning strengthened my resolve to seek other help. I obviously could not look after myself and was in no shape in mind, body, or spirit to look after my daughter, but deciding to go back to England to stay with my mother was one of the hardest and yet most obviously right decisions I had ever or have ever since made in my life. After heart-wrenching goodbyes at the airport, I somehow managed to travel alone back to England weighing barely eighty pounds.

My family was shocked and angry with me and wanted to have me hospitalized and forced fed, but I managed to persuade them to leave me alone for the time being. Living at home with Mum was a shockingly nerve-racking environment. My darling mother tottered around the uncarpeted part of the house in her steel-reinforced heeled shoes. The highbred sheltie dog she had was kept inside mostly and barked incessantly at any passerby. As her house was right next to an ever-increasingly traveled pathway and main road out of town, there was little peace.

I felt I needed to be in my own space and asked my grandmother if I could convert the old rock garden hut situated at the far end of the seven acres of gardens and the edge of the woods that she also owned. She put in a small AGA (European wood- or coal-burning, cast-iron stove, which is especially good at warming up a damp place with radiant heat and also can be used as a cookstove). She also installed a propane cooking stove, and my brother-in-law installed a wood floor to get me off the cold flagstones base. North Yorkshire has a very damp, cold climate, and even in summer, it can be a miserably cold place. I struggled to get peaceful within my body, initially feeling so grateful to be in my own space and in this serene and beautiful setting in nature.

I continued to practice yoga in the mornings and walking in the woods and fields daily. With no indoor bathroom, I just used a potty or squatted outside. I cooked vegetables and grains and ate slowly and carefully, chewing everything well in the way that was now so natural, but I was always hungry. And after eating a meal, I would search for something else that, once eaten, would invariably trigger pain and then I would end up purging myself of it all.

Sometimes I would go a few days with no reaction and feel so relieved but then I would eat something again that set off the cycle of binging and purging. I was getting more and more desperate, fearful, lonely, and prayed and cried for help from the universe. My health was slowly but surely deteriorating, and eventually, when the weather started to get really cold, I had to abandon my little retreat and went back to Mum's house by the road. Anyone who knew me that I saw in those days had tears in their eyes at the sight of this once-healthy, vibrant young woman who now looked like all the photos of starving people in third-world countries.

My younger sister once got furious and shouted at me, saying, "You're killing us with your wish to get attention."

I looked her in the eye and calmly said, "You don't understand what a nightmare my life is. I don't know what to eat. I have such discomfort in my body, and I am not doing it on purpose."

I asked her if she would be screaming at me if it was cancer that I had instead of an eating disorder, to which she replied, "No." So I asked her to try and have more compassion for this disease because I definitely didn't ask for or want to have it. In that moment, she realized that I was speaking the truth and she became my best friend and ally after that.

Chapter 20

Struggling to Stay Alive and Miracle Appointment

During those months that I was staying with my mother, I would occasionally find a certain food that would send a wonderful feeling of energy and well-being down my spine. It would circulate through my body as I was guided to eat it. So I would keep eating this magic food until it no longer produced that effect, and I would once again get seriously depressed and withdrawn. At one point, I ate deep-fried, pounded sweet rice dumplings called *mochi* daily for six weeks until it began to taste disgusting.

Then I began to shut down. I barely spoke and didn't laugh, cry, sneeze, or even cough. I still loved to walk and remained strong in that way. But climbing stairs was starting to be difficult, as my knees were often hot, red, and puffy, and there were signs that my system was under tremendous pressure. And there was a yellow tinge to my skin color. It is interesting that I nowadays use this phrase, under pressure, to describe exactly what was the case. It was 1989, and I was thirty-two. Rose, who was by then thirteen, was living in the United States of America with Ben at weekends and my friend Mourka during the week because I simply wasn't able to take care of her.

Rose came to England for a visit during the summer holidays, and it was an extremely hard emotional time. I had started seeing a therapist twice a week, Sue Holden, who had taught the introductory tai chi class the previous summer. Sue helped me in so many ways and especially to understand how the pathology of parents is inadvertently passed onto the children in various guises. Rose came with me to meet her during her summer visit and had a couple of sessions alone with her, which I believe was vitally important for her. Sue supported me all through that year and some years to follow, and I am eternally grateful to her for her steady, clear wisdom; insights; and wonderful, strong spiritual energy.

I went down to London to the East-West Center on two different occasions to seek the advice and shiatsu treatment of a macrobiotic counselor whom I had met previously when visiting United Kingdom. On the second visit, he said that he had to be honest and say that he couldn't help me further—that I was gravely ill and perhaps my only chance to heal using the macrobiotic way was to get a consultation with Denny Waxman, a senior macrobiotic counselor who specialized in eating disorders and who was now living in Portugal with his wife and children.

He said that Denny Waxman would be visiting London to give consultations in the middle of October but that I would need to see if there was an opening available because he was often fully booked. I spoke to the receptionist and found that he was indeed fully booked but was told that if I left my phone number, someone would call if there was a cancelation and subsequent opening to see him. It was already the beginning of October.

Whilst taking the train back up to Yorkshire, I was now feeling that I simply had to see Denny Waxman, that he was my last chance, and that if I didn't, I was probably going to die.

As luck would have it, the call came about a week later and I was filled with a sense of hope, a strong feeling, and blind faith that I was going to enter a time of great change that was both exciting and very scary. A few months afterward, I also had great gratitude to the person who had canceled because it saved my life and I hoped that person was also somehow okay.

A dear friend, Angel, who was living in Bristol, traveled up to London and took me under her wing. She met me off the train from

Yorkshire, accepting me just as I was, which was likely a pretty scary sight. She got us a taxi, and we went to see Denny Waxman for a consultation at the East-West Center, seven months after my first attempt to see him.

He had fortuitously forgotten my phone call back in March. He calmly diagnosed me, using oriental technique of checking the pulses and heat/damp in certain meridians, tongue, hands/palms, and feet/ankles. When done, he sat down and then told me that the reason for my condition was that my mother had eaten lots of cheese, chicken, and eggs during her pregnancy with me. He was the first person to say that I had severe hypoglycemia. He was also the first person to tell me that I was a highly sensitive person. Even though I didn't fully understand what he meant, a knowing light bulb went off and I just knew that all that he said was in fact true. I was completely open and ready to hear everything he said. The timing apparently was perfect.

In the hour that I was with him, I began to realize the truth of my present condition and became aware of all that I'd been doing wrong to exacerbate it. I realized that the constricted physical condition of my organs, especially the pancreas and spleen, had been causing me to think and behave in a tight way, choosing foods that kept making me more contracted and tight. Denny went through an entire pamphlet of recipes and lifestyle recommendations, while Angel took notes on another form for clarity, and a three-month food plan was laid out with the suggestion that I see him again for a follow-up visit when he was next in London.

He suggested that I try and hire a qualified macrobiotic cook to help me get started and supplied a few contacts. I remember telling him that I had discovered a way to feel really peaceful and that was through fasting, and he replied that now it was time to make and find peace with eating food. Angel and I ate lunch afterward at the East-West / Community Health Foundation macrobiotic restaurant. I was usually very nervous about eating out but on this occasion, strangely had a confidence that I was in a safe place and even stopped eating lunch halfway through, feeling satisfied but ready for the pudding dessert. And it all tasted so delicious, the first balanced meal that I had eaten in years that didn't give me pain or make me feel uncomfortable and wanting to purge. I felt high and so optimistic and hopeful.

Then we did a big shop next door at the Clearspring Natural Grocers for all the foods that Denny Waxman had recommended and that I was unable to get in Yorkshire. I decided that I probably would not have a lot of extra time to prepare some of the more laborious foods that I had got in the habit of making myself, so I decided to stock up on ready-made amazake, natto, and seitan. Angel read down the list as we walked around filling up the cart with beautiful organic produce and Japanese/macrobiotic foods.

Afterward, we went back to stay a few nights in Angel's London flat. I read over the notes, and even though I was overwhelmed by all that I was going to need to do, I had a whole new feeling of hope, optimism, and excitement. The next morning, I cooked some leftover rice very softly with big chunks of sweet Hokkaido winter squash and plenty of water. The first mouthful tasted like nectar, mother's milk. That's the message I got then, and every mouthful afterward soothed and relaxed my poor, starving, tortured body, mind, and soul/spirit. Without really understanding but with a blind belief, I just knew I was onto something very special and healing.

During the time of that first meeting with Denny Waxman at the East-West Center in London, something in me changed in a very forceful way. An extraordinary and profound shift in consciousness emerged and seemed to fill my empty old self. I was filled with a deep humility, compassion, empathy, and gratitude for all and everything. I immediately became aware that, contrary to my victim-oriented thinking that every problem in my life was caused by inadequate parenting, I realized that my parents were key components in helping me on my life journey and that it was up to me to find out how to heal and become my essential self. I birthed a daughter as an under-developed young woman and now saw that she, too, was an integral part of my journey. I began to understand that all beings on the planet are here to help each other.

My mother and grandmother straight away became my biggest support. When I returned from my visit to see Denny Waxman, the first thing my mother said was "I know you're going to get better now." My grandmother said, "Something has changed in you, and I feel hopeful." The whole family had wanted to put me into a rehabilitation facility, and I now asked them to give me six months to see if Denny's recommendations could help change my condition.

The macrobiotic philosophy was special and made such sense to me, and I sensed that if I began to nourish myself appropriately and accurately, I had a better chance of survival. I knew my illness was from a deep-rooted condition from before birth, but it never entered my mind to blame either my mother or grandmother or any other relatives or ancestors. On the contrary, I actually started to understand the family condition better and that I had been born through it. I didn't want a quick fix but rather, to heal the symptoms from the root cause. My mother and grandmother somehow knew I was speaking a truth, and I began to have a wonderful relationship with both of them from that day forward. After all, they trusted me.

Chapter 21

Beginning to Treat the Condition

Even though Denny Waxman had recommended that I hire a cook, I was unable to find someone who was available to travel up to that out-of-the-way part of North Yorkshire, so I did it all on my own. In a way, I actually think that this was fortunate, as I believe it helped me have a much better understanding of my condition. I was, above all, most fortunate to have the luxury of staying with my mother, and all the time, I needed to concentrate on healing myself.

Denny had given me a list of ten lifestyle steps (now it has been formatted to be seven) that he strongly suggested I practice to help strengthen my health and these included: twice-daily body rub; half-hour daily walk; having regular meals and eating in an orderly manner, always sitting down; not mixing foods on the plate and chewing everything very well; eating balanced daily meals by always including a grain, vegetable, and soup; wearing only cotton material next to skin; cooking on a flame stove; making inside of the home as natural as possible (i.e., no synthetic carpets, mattress, minimizing electric gadgets, etc.); having plants in each room in the house; being active; practicing hobbies; and above all, being grateful for all.

Well, I had already discovered the art and pleasure of eating/chewing well, which, luckily for me, I now had plenty of practice. I simply couldn't swallow anything until it was liquid along with sitting to eat quietly without doing anything else, but I then began to include saying prayers beforehand, giving thanks to all. Daily walking came naturally as did wearing natural/cotton clothing and having plants in the house along with hobbies and gratitude. Creating balanced meals was my new challenge, but I seemed to get the hang of it as time went on.

Denny had said that the body rub was a very important and part of my regimen as it would help move stagnant energy and improve my circulation. I didn't question this idea, just sensing that it was maybe one of the best things I could do for myself.

Interestingly enough, this was actually also not such a new idea to me. At boarding school, there were no showers, only baths and washbasins. As there were almost seven hundred students to keep clean, we were only allowed a bath or to wash our hair once a week. And every morning and evening, the washbasins were half filled by the matrons with tepid water and we had to give ourselves bird baths using a cotton facecloth.

So my daily regimen now included the Denny Waxman macrobiotic-style body rub as a vital practice that Denny said was to be done twice a day, first thing in the morning and last thing in the evening and continuously for the rest of my life.

This is the recipe for that simple, life-changing practice.

I was instructed to fill up a sink or bowl with hot water. The warmer the water the better the results. Then I had to take a 100 percent cotton washcloth, dip it into the water, and squeeze out the excess water. Then starting with my face and neck, start gently but firmly rubbing my entire body skin surface, paying special attention in between fingers, toes, and lymph nodes under the arms and groin area and doing a clever little maneuver, continuously redipping the washcloth in the water and squeezing out the excess. This ritual took/takes about fifteen to twenty minutes.

There is absolutely no doubt in my mind and body that this body rub is one of the most vitally important ingredients to regaining and ever since, maintaining my health. The warmth of the wet washcloth serves to relax and open the skin pores. The rubbing motion serves to help move old or stagnant energy, increases blood flow, and reactivates the meridians, duplicating our journey down the birth canal and subsequently being constantly caressed, cared for, and generally touched as babies and children. As we age, there is generally a decline in this activity. The body rub is a simple and pure act of reactivation and self-love.

Those early days of standing in the bathroom with a small electric bar heater pointed toward my shivering emaciated body are still etched clearly in my memory. I also wasn't to have any baths and only to have a very short warm shower once a week. This was to avoid making my body too hot, as I could not afford to sweat out vital minerals and then be craving salt, which I needed to keep to a minimum in order to avoid a contracting effect, especially to the spleen and pancreas, which needed all the relaxation they could get.

Since then, I have made some personal add-ons, which I was naturally inclined to include. Once the basin or bowl is filled with hot water, I place the first hot, wrung-out washcloth over my back kidney area for a minute and then proceed with the full-body rub. At the end, I place one foot at a time in the water to warm up my feet. These two additions make the process more complete for me.

The new shift in my state of mind and being began to escalate as each new day dawned. I would go to bed at night after doing the body rub and say thank-you for having being given the opportunity to become a better person in mind, body, and spirit and that it was okay if I died that night because I had lived through and experienced one more day in which to better understand and heal my deep-rooted family/birth/root condition. I then slept on my back in a deeply relaxed sleep. When I first awakened in the morning, it was to find myself in exactly the same position, on my back, still in my body, alive and breathing.

I was filled with an ever-deepening sense of wonder, gratitude, and excitement at what this/that new day would bring. I was in awe at the miracle of life and aware that I was actually really experiencing it, maybe for the first time. I was guided to speak and behave in a certain way. There was only room for gratitude, love, and this strong blind faith of somehow knowing that I was doing the right and best thing for myself in order to heal. I would hear no malice or gossip against another, feeling (my) life energy was too precious to waste on such things. I only saw the beauty and condition of each and every person and felt great empathy and compassion for all.

Several books with powerful messages seemed to just show up one after the other. One of the books that I had bought several years before when I had first started my macrobiotic practice of chewing was *The Book of Do-In* by Michio Kushi. Back then, I had opened the book, read the first sentence, which reads, "In the beginning-less beginning, the universe did not manifest as phenomena," and promptly shut the book, feeling immediately overwhelmed by the enormity of that idea. The funny thing is that as I traveled between countries during the previous few years, I actually carried that book around with me as though it had an important message somehow.

And then, lo and behold, when I returned from seeing Denny Waxman, I found myself drawn to this book again. This time, however, as I read that first sentence again, now nearly three years on since buying it, the words made perfect sense. Of course. The "beginning-less beginning." What else could it be? And as I read the entire book, I was filled more and more with what I call a sense of knowing and grace. I started practicing the Do-In morning and evening exercises and learned the meaning of what we commonly call the vowel sounds and three particular chants, all of which I draw on to this day whenever I am called to at any given moment. Other books included biographies on Krishna Murti, Mother Teresa, and Gandhi; *The Practice of the Presence of God* by Brother Lawrence; translations of the *Rubaiyat* of Omar Khayyam and the *Bhagavad Gita*; *The Prophecy* by Khalil Gibran; and *The Tibetan Book of Living and Dying*. All these beautiful wise tomes served to nourish my spirit/soul, hungry for truth, wisdom, and earthly human enlightenment.

I also still maintained my daily practice of morning yoga and meditation and started to add some prayers of gratitude. Each and every day, I renewed (and continue to renew ever since) my pledge and commitment to healing myself through the study and practice of macrobiotics and the consideration of all things that I might become a better person in mind, body, and spirit and more and more my essential self. I prayed most earnestly that I could let go, be free, be healthy, and at peace to do the will of God in all things and at all times in the service of others. I prayed to know and love myself better that I could also know and love others in return totally and unconditionally.

I made a promise as each day dawned and I awoke that if I could heal myself using this method, I would always try and help others in this way as it had saved/restored my life. Actually, I felt I was really being reborn—that with everything I ate and did, a fresh, new energy was being created within me. I was emerging slowly from being the caterpillar to becoming a butterfly.

I was very aware that I had spent so much time and energy in the past years trying to find what foods were good or best for me, and now that I had been given a custom-made formula and diet, I would need to use that energy to learn how to accurately prepare it all. And boy, did I need plenty of energy to prepare all the dishes freshly daily. You could say I had my plate full in all ways. I was excited to get going as the food was delicious and satisfying, but I was also constantly hungry because I was so undernourished and so I had a lot of catching up to do.

Also, because I had been eating in such a narrow or tight way, the new, gentle, soft, relaxing, uplifting foods began to loosen me up in all ways and I was constantly in the loo. Hence, it was a seemingly never-ending cycle of cooking, washing up, eating, and eliminating all day long. But during those first few months, I did not have one single anorexic or bulimic moment, and this was a great miracle. The nightmare that I had been living for the past years began to ease, and I was living, sleeping deeply, and awaking with a renewed sense of calm and well-being.

I began to experience and learn what foods made me feel good and which ones didn't. I had picked up a book by Krystina Turner, and in it, she suggested that in order to get a better understanding of the energy of foods, one could do a little taste test using carrots prepared or cooked in three different ways. One was to be long cooked in water, the second one to be lightly steamed, and the third one to be grated raw. The long-cooked one seemed to go deeply into my body and made me feel warm and comforted, the crunchiness of the lightly steamed one made me feel peppy and energetic, and the grated raw carrot made me feel very light and cooler still.

It was so very helpful and equipped me with a new way of really beginning to understand the energetic nature of foods. In those early days, I felt my life depended on my being very accurate, but I was also coming from such a tight place that I occasionally misinterpreted some of the recommendations. For instance, Denny Waxman suggested that for my main grain dishes that I cook brown rice together with another grain plus a sweet vegetable and also millet with a sweet vegetable. I thought he meant I was exclusively to have only these grain mixtures and hence, for the first six months, ate only these combination three times a day. However, I eventually realized that one of the key factors in creating good, healthy, balanced meals and therefore good health is by incorporating a wide variety of foods, styles, and dishes on a regular and daily basis.

Denny Waxman had said to avoid bread and oil, except for adding a few drops to a particular arame seaweed with vegetables dish. Gradually, I learned to enjoy pressed and blanched salads, daily steamed greens, steamed fruit, and a delicious traditional Japanese fermented sweet rice pudding or drink called amazake once or twice a week. I had miso soup twice a day, drinking only the broth, to avoid ingesting the salt-infused vegetables. Rice always had to be soaked in advance and cooked with another grain and a sweet vegetable. I had two bowls of rice cream daily as in-between meal snacks along with two cups of sweet vegetable drink and a few unsalted almonds. I slowly came to understand my underlying condition of hypoglycemia, the original state that had manifested into bulimia and anorexia, how it had manifested, and how it was beginning to be healed. It was a brilliant realization.

Basically, it is my understanding that because I had been born with a compromised, contracted pancreas and spleen and insulin was not being produced and/or excreted into the bloodstream with any regularity, I was dependent on very sweet tastes to trigger insulin secretion. The fact that the first food that I accepted at birth was sugar-sweetened cow's milk now gave me a much clearer understanding of the tightness of those organs and of the constant seesawing of anorexia and bulimia that had plagued me for so long. I was now working on strengthening my pancreatic and spleen function by eating mildly sweet tastes on a regular basis and most especially making sure that I had regular meal times and at the best times to align with all the organs functions.

After my chewing-for-the-first-time experience, I had begun practicing macrobiotics intellectually by trying to apply a sugar/dairy/animal-food-free diet without realizing that I was further exacerbating my condition and this especially included the contraction of my kidneys, which began to make me very fearful of food/eating and overworked my liver. Then began a vicious cycle/pattern of behavior that is a common one in so many people: By taking away a common food that sustained, I then contracted to a place of fear and would be afraid to eat and then get so hungry that I would eat extreme foods that made me in turn feel so full that I thought I would have a heart attack. And the only relief was to purge myself, and on and on it would go.

Anyway, in those early days of healing, I would wake at 5:00 a.m., shocked to still be alive. Once I got over the shock, I would give thanks to have been given another chance to be in the world in a better way. I did my morning body rub and cooked the previously soaked breakfast grain and rice cream cereal for snacks, miso soup, and steamed vegetables for the first meal of the day. Then I went and did yoga in my bedroom, made my bed, and cleaned the room. Then I took my early morning walk, barefoot when possible, before having breakfast. Those walks were very special. Several months earlier, I had noticed that I was somehow tasting and drinking my breath as I inhaled the fragrant and often-humid air. So now, after a few months of practicing/experiencing this, I came upon a chapter in the book of Do-In that included this as one of the suggested spiritual practices called drinking the heavenly dew.

I also included—and still do—hugging a tree and giving thanks to my parents (my father's tree energy and my mother's earth energy) for my life and being alive still. After breakfast, I would then start to prepare food for lunch and so the days would go. It generally took me five hours to prepare my daily food and another five to eat it. I would make sure that I had all my meals at the same regular times, chewing well. And each meal lasted about an hour and a half and snacks took about fifteen through twenty minutes.

Denny had said that it would be good to keep a journal of all that I ate and felt for those first few months. The first thing I wrote in it was "I feel that I am my own mother and child in this body, teaching myself, learning to eat, live, nourish, and nurture myself properly for the first time." I also noted how I was in the habit of smelling everything before I cooked or ate it and how wonderful it felt to have my senses being so active and alive. I was being fed by my ability to smell, touch, taste, and eventually, feel.

My darling mother did much of my everyday shopping in the early days, carrying large bags of vegetables and grains up a steep hill from the town. It was very challenging to be living with her, as she was quite hyper and her sheltie dog, which wasn't allowed outside on her own, was constantly barking at the passersby and anyone who came to visit. But it was also a real blessing to be together with her during this time. Before I had the consultation with Denny Waxman, I used to question my mother's alcohol consumption (which was fairly prolific, as I had discreetly marked the bottles) and this made her nervous and drink more. Now I realized that she also had a deep condition of hypoglycemia, and we had a lot more in common than I had ever known. So now, when I saw Mummy downing gin and tonics or whiskey, I no longer worried about her, as I realized it was her way of keeping balance with the large amounts of animal and salty foods.

She actually began to drink less while I was with her, but also, sadly for her, she stopped going to attend all her various hobbies, including her beloved Scottish dancing evenings. It was not until a few years later that my younger sister told me that Mummy stopped going out because she feared I might be dead when she got back and wanted to keep a vigil at my side. I began to have real heart-to-heart conversations with her, and I genuinely had a new interest in her life and what she had experienced growing up and therefore began to have greater compassion and empathy.

I always offered Mummy some of the food I cooked, but she would eat only three of my dishes: breakfast oats with lots of rice syrup sweetener, blanched cauliflower, broccoli and radish salad, and blanched watercress with red radish and sweet corn salad. A few weeks into my healing, I was standing next to the stove and gently toasting a piece of nori seaweed under the top grill. I offered Mum to try a piece, and she said, "No, thank you, darling. It smells like rabbit poo." And we both started laughing, I for the first time in many, many months. Mummy came up, hugged me, and said with tears in her eyes that she was so happy to see me laugh and she just knew I was going to get better. It was a special moment.

During this time of being with Mum at the family home and interacting with my siblings and grandmother on a daily basis, I saw more clearly the hypoglycemic connection that we all shared and how it manifested in a variety of symptoms. I also realized that there could be no blame whatsoever to my parents, mother, father, or grandparents (nor indeed their ancestors before them) for this family condition, as everyone was just doing the best they knew how to do at the time. I felt a greater gratitude toward them for all they had been through before me. If not for them and how they lived and suffered, I would not have come to this point in understanding. The old me seemed to have blamed all my troubles on what my parents did or didn't do, when in fact, it was up to me to use their gift of giving life in any way I chose. Now I was choosing a new and wonderful way of living, and I was filled with great love and gratitude to them. They had surely helped me become who I was becoming.

I usually joined the family for lunch at my grandmothers', once or twice a week, bringing a grain, bean, and salad dish to substitute the inevitable potatoes and meat that were served and had been a staple of my childhood diet. I noticed how all the sweet root vegetables, like Swedish turnips, rutabagas called swedes, and carrots or parsnips were boiled to death with lots of (table/rock) salt in my grandmother's kitchen and then all the delicious sweet boiling water poured down the sink and huge pieces of farm butter mixed in at the end.

I suggested to the cook, Mrs. Bell, to eliminate nearly all the salt and to save some of the water that would normally be discarded so everyone could taste the sweet water. Mrs. Bell happily started to use less water and salt and didn't pour away the water at the end, and she also reduced butter at the end to a small portion so that I could enjoy the vegetables with everyone and comply with Denny Waxman's recommendations.

With each new day that I was gifted, I slowly began to really understand and get to know who I am and that I was somehow becoming more and more my essential self. I realized that my being disciplined, strong-willed, and determined were some of my natural traits and served to help me get through this great challenge of healing and saving myself.

I also realized that one of my very strong natural instincts/traits is my sensuality. That is to say I love to connect fully with everything through smell, taste, touch, and sound naturally without aforethought. I automatically smell any food item before starting to cook with it—to breathe in the aroma of anything that I was/am about to eat and things in nature when out walking.

My practice of walking outdoors barefooted—weather permitting—that was already in place, became ever more meaningful and beneficial in feeling the ground beneath me and connecting to the earth. Hearing a pair of owls hooting in conversation and the sound of the rain or wind in the trees became wonderful new gifts. The sweet scent of a downy baby bird feather or a large one dropped by a hawk have their own unique heavenly scent. Each tree that I hugged gave me the gift of its sweet or musky sap scent. Every single scent and sound became messengers with important information.

I remember especially the revelation that occurred when I discovered having an energetic experience when I simply smelled two different miso pastes in an effort to choose which one to use that day. The message was clearly a yes or a no, and the choices of anything became easier and easier from then on. So much so that nowadays, I will get the yes-or-no message without even smelling first, as I now get a feeling in my hara/abdominal area that determines what is right when faced with any options that require a choice.

I began to realize the extent of my sensitivity and sensuality and how important it was that I knew this about myself. All the time I had been seeking peaceful, serene, quiet places to be suddenly made perfect sense. I also began to have a better understanding of the fact that there are many people on this earth who simply don't know who they are and what or how to give themselves what they need in order to either just survive or live comfortably. Being a sensitive person can be both a blessing and a curse, depending on self-awareness and the tools we have to help us.

Another interesting thing happened during this time. One day, I walked into what was called the smoking room at Saint Nicholas to find MM sitting in her usual armchair, knitting and watching TV news, as she was accustomed to doing in the late afternoon. I had this strong sense of her wanting to have her shoulders massaged. I stopped myself asking her at first, but the feeling was so clear, and when I finally found my voice and courage, she said, "Oh, how wonderful. Would you really do that for me? My mother had a person come to give us both massage weekly, and I haven't had it since."

Well, that was the beginning of what would become an evening ritual between her and I and for the rest of her life whenever I was at home in the United Kingdom. I would seek her out in the kitchen where she was enjoying her whiskey and orange juice (her daily medicine prescribed by her doctor for stress and tension back in the seventies) and give twenty minutes of neck, shoulder, head, and back massage to which she would go into a blissfully relaxed place and purr like a cat. She knew when I was about to end our little session and said she wished it could go on and endlessly!

She was always so gentle, sweet, and grateful during those times together, and we became increasingly closer. I also used to give her manicures and pedicures if she was preparing for guests. In her last few years when she was often in bed for days at a time, I would instead give her feet similar attention. How amazing that—after all the times that she had rushed me to go faster, eat more quickly, and hurry up during my childhood years—she was then slowed down enough to receive and enjoy the benefit from this sharing born out of my healing that she totally supported me in and my natural slower pace.

After I first saw Denny Waxman, I actually lost weight, as my system opened up and at my lowest weighed seventy-five pounds. I had been constipated and hardly urinating. My newfound sweet baby food was so wonderful. Soft rice with squash tasted and felt like mother's milk to me. It was heaven. It was what I had been looking for my whole life. This soft, sweet, light food was exactly what I'd been craving and yet didn't know to have or how to prepare it. Apart from the rice cream cereal, which I made every other day, everything was prepared fresh daily for the first six months, and apart from some grain dishes, I ate no leftovers at all. The habit of chewing everything really well coupled with appropriate food for my better health began to show its best effectiveness, and slowly but surely, subtle physical, psychological, and spiritual changes began to manifest.

By giving my body, mind, and spirit what it really needed, rather than a diet dictated by conditioning and pathology, I began to slowly heal myself and in turn started to make wiser choices. This nurtured my true intuition to begin to work for me in everyday life choices.

There is no doubt that my essential authentic self began to emerge, and as I write this, thirty-two years later, it becomes ever more apparent. The more I nurture myself well and appropriately, the clearer my inner voice becomes and the easier it is to hear. This voice is not in my head or mind but rather, in my core being.

I also began to get messages from my food. Denny had suggested that I snack on unsalted almonds, and as I chewed the first one, I could feel its energy and that started to happen with everything I put into my mouth. I got messages of its energetic nature. I'd feel my energy dive or expand as I'd eat something. I'd know if it were contracting or relaxing, warming or cooling, strengthening or weakening, right away. I knew where it had come from, like the almond embedded in a strong, rooted tree, suspended on a branch, and housed in an incredibly hard shell surrounded by thin air. I got a clear sense of food. I became so calm that I could feel everything that came to me with its unique its information. This was another proof of the reason that I had been advised to not mix up the different food dishes on the plate in order to allow each specially prepared dish give its message and greatest impact/benefit. It's so cool!

It was also during that time that I started to view all in the world simply as having human condition in any given moment in time. I began to understand that what we eat/ingest affects our thinking and behavior. I sensed that if every human being learned from an early age to eat a spiritually based diet customized for their own condition, there would be peace and great good health on earth.

I also began to notice that some of my tendencies were so connected to both my extremely sensitive nature but also my condition. When I'm too yang/tight, it becomes harder and harder to stop what I am doing. I'll feel like I need to finish something before I can relax or change direction.

The whole experience continually becomes more and more extraordinary. I see the miracle of life, movement, and energy. Often, I can sense energy moving through my body. I feel myself to be a moving mass with my spirit hovering. Sometimes I feel huge as if I am the universe. Other times, I feel like the tiniest of atoms.

The voice within was very strong, guiding me to make better choices for myself and to understand my condition better. It was the voice of survival but also the emergence and survival of my authentic self. MM had always been very controlling and had no time for selfishness, but as I began to heal and get more in touch with what I needed, I was able to take the time I needed to look after myself, prioritize self-care, and set healthy boundaries. I became my own mother and child, learning to care for myself properly for the first time in my life. Being selfish had a whole new meaning. It was no longer a bad thing when used in this way, and the new personal lifestyle was really suiting me.

In between all the cooking, cleaning, and eating, I spent a great deal of time sewing and knitting all sorts of clothing and gifts for Rose, the family, and friends. I collected sheep's wool that had gotten stuck on brambles and shrubs in MM's fields and washed, carded, and hand spun it and then began to knit squares to make a blanket (a story of the history of this blanket to follow).

During those eleven months that I was in England, I journeyed down to the South of England and stayed with Angel and her family for a few weeks in Bristol, then onto to my cousin Nadia in Devon and afterward to my macrobiotic mentor / Carpet Bags / Green Desert friends, Harry and Loretta. The variety of location, environment, and friends really helped to further shift my stuck energy and to also break up the intensity of being with my mother and giving her a break from my intensity and generally seeing so much of the rest of the family on a regular basis. There was renewed appreciation for all upon my return.

Chapter 22

Return to USA

By late spring of 1990, I knew it was time to leave my mother's home again and to go back to the United States to be with Rose for the summer holidays. And so I did, and it was a very special time to be reunited with her again. I had my second appointment with Denny Waxman during that summer and invited Rose and her girlfriend to come with me, and that was the beginning of my really sharing the newfound health and lifestyle with her. Now that I was understanding better how to feed myself, it helped me to understand better how to feed and what to offer her. Rose was born through my birth condition, so she had no doubt inherited and been influenced by this.

It was so very hard leaving my daughter in the United States of America. When we were reunited, she gradually began to notice the change in me, liked the food I was cooking, and usually tasted everything I offered. Before, my food had been dry and salty, and even though she had favorite dishes that I had taken care to provide, much of the food I had cooked for myself she wasn't interested in and rightly so. She had become a well-adapted young woman. Now she was more trusting and would ask me for advice when needed. She began to notice the beneficial difference that this new way of cooking could manifest and from then on, would seek out healthy/healthier food when she had colds or felt unwell and generally strayed too far into the tempting world of highly stimulating sweets and dairy/animal foods.

Even though I was considerably better and stronger, I was still very underweight, and Denny Waxman had suggested then that I possibly spend the upcoming winter in a warmer climate to further help relax my condition. So I bought an old car for $400 and as luck would have it, on the same day, met some people in the local health shop who offered me to stay in their home down in Sarasota, Florida, while I looked for a suitable rental.

That journey I took on my own was quite extraordinary. I had bought a little one-burner Le Blue butane camping stove and packed a few pots and pans, cooking utensils, and chopping board. I packed a big, hard cooler with plenty of ice and some perishable foods and a couple of boxes with jars of grains and beans, set off one morning after breakfast, and drove until it was time to eat lunch and then again until it was time to stop and cook supper and retire for the night. I was very careful to eat on a regular schedule and gave myself plenty of time to allow for all the rituals that were my vital foundation, such as doing the body rub, having a half-hour walk, and preparing all the food needed for the day.

In the latest consultation, Denny had also suggested to have occasional leftovers now, so I made extra food at supper to have for lunch the next day along with a different precooked grain. This self-reliance was very new to me and added to the confidence that seemed to be building daily as I learned how to look after myself on all levels of life. For that first year, I saw him every six months and then once a year for about three years. Nowadays, I see him when needed, for food adjustments, or 9 Star Ki consultations.

It was on one of my visits to see Denny Waxman—after returning from an energetically challenging trip to the United Kingdom in 1994—that he introduced me to an ancient Japanese astrology/cosmology system based on the five elements (fire, water, wood, metal, soil) called 9 Star Ki. And from that point on, he began to give me useful directional suggestions to help me place myself on the planet that would give the most supportive energy. This ancient system helped me to know myself better and embrace my natural traits, which aren't seen as good or bad. Rather, they are the front and the back, the yin and the yang, the expanded and the contracted sides of each and every being. As a metal energy person, my natural traits include on the one hand being hypersensitive, easygoing, sociable, and talented. And on the other hand, I am calculating, stubborn, self-assertive, and persistent. It is an ongoing interest as I continue getting to know more about who I am (becoming). I have been studying and using the system ever since finding it so very interesting and energetically helpful in areas of movement and travel.

I found a perfect little downtown apartment close to where I had lived years before and was allowed to take up the carpet to reveal lovely old wood floors. I bought a bicycle (which I am sorry to say was stolen in the first week outside the health food shop that I had shopped at for the years we had lived there, never having to worry about it being stolen back then; times had changed).

I started making quilts out of recycled fabrics. I was able to acquire outdated upholstery swatch books from a couple of the local interior designer shops and scoured the charity and thrift shops for nice tablecloths for the backings and wool blankets for the linings. I sold a few at a local craft fair and also began making some jewelry. I was in the habit of making clothing for my daughter and kept busy on the latest request she had made for her upcoming birthday and Easter gifts. I connected with a woman called Delia Quigley, who was listed in the macrobiotic directory I had bought as being the founder of the Macrobiotic Society of Sarasota and who has ever since been a dear friend. She became a huge support, accepting my silence when I ate, hiring me to help do vegetable preparation work for the man for whom she was cooking at the time, and we hung out together often.

She humbled me once when we were walking along the beach after a morning spent cooking and sharing a quiet lunch. She had asked me if she could video me telling my story and on this occasion, had not in fact brought her camera but was asking me about my childhood spent with my grandmother. I began to speak in the old poor-me/victim kind of voice, and after a few minutes, Delia asked me to stop for a moment and very firmly but kindly validated and empathized with me but said she was rather tired of hearing this sorry-for-myself dialogue.

I was instantly made aware of how boring it was. And ever since that day, I have been grateful to her for sharing so honestly. I have used this as an example when anyone, whom I know well and care about, begins to do the poor-me voice and it works every time to bring them to a place of truth and gratitude.

I arranged for Rose to come and stay with me in Florida for the Christmas holidays and to coincide with my mother also coming from the United Kingdom. Mummy was very happy to see me better, albeit in spirit more than physically, for I had not yet gained much weight. We had bonded over the eleven months that I healed in her home, as I was able to really treasure her for the first time. Mummy had been afraid of swimming for many years since being pushed into a pool once, but I coaxed her into the warm, calm waters of the Gulf of Mexico and held her as she floated and began to swim. She was radiant, laughing, and so happy to be in the sea after many years, and once again, we shared a new closeness and I felt such gratitude for our time together.

Ben and I usually kept in touch weekly. And one day, he called to say that he needed to get a divorce so that he was free to marry a woman he had recently met, and that was done fairly quickly without too much hesitation. And I wished him well. I hoped we would remain friends, especially for the sake of our daughter.

As the weeks went by, I began to slowly put on some weight, and as spring arrived, I knew that it was time to return to New York to be with my daughter again, who was still living during the weekdays with the newly divorced Mourka and her two children and spending weekends with her dad and his new lady in the house we owned in Rosendale, New York.

Chapter 23

Living with My New Family in Upstate New York 1993–1996

Upon arriving back to my old home territory, Mourka invited me to stay with her and so I moved in with my two fruit boxes filled with jars of grains, beans, and pressure cooker. Initially, there was no extra bedroom, so I slept on the sofa, which I seem to remember was regularly used as a trampoline in the day by Mourka's son and his friends!

We entered into a really wonderful and nurturing relationship. I became the housewife, and while Mourka was gone most days, teaching, I would cook and take care of all the household chores. As the stove was electric, I would prepare much of my food on the little propane camping burners that I used for traveling. Mourka and her children were used to eating quite differently. However, she often cooked delicious authentic Russian dishes, and we began to happily share our foods. Rose would sit and eat first with me and when she had had enough of my food and silent eating, would then go and sit and eat with Mourka and the children. Mourka often said how much she loved eating the macrobiotic dishes, and it was a pleasure to witness some of the healing power of my newfound diet and lifestyle working its magic on subtle levels.

Living with them all was one of the most healing and fun time I had ever experienced. Mourka had quite a few close friends and Russian relatives who would visit and/or stay. There was a lot of laughter and love, and I began to steadily put on more weight and to feel really well and truly alive. I used to bicycle to the High Falls Co-op once a week and during the hotter months, often went down to the river to swim. I remember on one occasion finding two rolls of quarters on my way back from a swim. The local theatre had a $2 movie night special, so after supper, we all went to see a film funded by the find.

Picking up being mother to my daughter, Rose, had its challenges. She had gone through several times of being separated from me, and understandably, she was wary of getting too close or comfortable, lest I suddenly leave again. However, as the weeks progressed, I was able to do more and more with her and to join in with some of her school projects. She was enrolled with a wonderful dance program with a company called the Vanaver Caravan. This meant ferrying her to rehearsals.

I also helped in the preparation of the huge barn that was used for the summer dance festival, and it turned out that the dancers in her class were in need of new costumes, alterations, and repairs and I was hired as their new costumier and thoroughly enjoyed once again being back in the swing of things and life. My gratitude grew daily.

I was still working on healing, cleansing, and strengthening my health and also had not had a monthly menstrual cycle since 1986. And so I checked in with Denny Waxman again, making the trip into New York City for the day, and he gave new recommendations to further open me up, which were always so interesting, delicious, and helpful. He suggested incorporating a few new food dishes and also that I start playing table tennis or badminton. The idea behind the latter was that by practicing a not-too-overly-exerting sport in which energy is exchanged, I might help stimulate my reproductive system to be activated.

Denny Waxman said that if none of these ideas worked, he recommended that I seek out a good Chinese herbalist for a tea remedy. It just so happened that Mourka had both a badminton set and table tennis and I happily began playing games with the whole family.

In addition, I had begun to spend some time with a rather wonderful musician and after a night together, awoke the next morning finding my moon cycle had restarted. I was over the moon and felt like a teenager who had just started her menses for the first time. I thanked my lover and the universe for once again giving me the gift of health and life. My inner voice instructed me to be very quiet and peaceful for the four days that I had my flow, and I was filled with grace and gratitude. From then on until I went through menopause, my monthly cycles were a great and wonderful blessing and I miss them still. The quiet time that I spent at home for the four days of flow were so very peaceful, and I felt more and more connected to the natural source of the planet and the universe.

During these times, my body instructed me to not do yoga, heavy lifting, or cleaning and to do very little socializing. The flow would stop if I drove or exerted myself, so I usually didn't go anywhere or get into any big conversations. A few months later, a friend of Mourka's—to whom I had told my story—lent me a book called *The Red Tent*, which tells the story of how, in past ages, the menstruating women in the Middle East went into a special tent where they were waited on by the elders. No work of any kind was permitted once they entered the tent, and their flow went straight into the earth. It seemed I was naturally guided to allow this ancient ritual. Later on in the summer, Rose invited me to join her in a workshop celebrating women's rite of passage, which helped to bring some healing between us in a powerful way as I had been in the United Kingdom struggling with my health and absent when she began her moon cycles.

When I returned to the United Kingdom in the winter for Christmas and I shared the news of my newly begun menses with MM, she was very happy for me and said that when she was on her moons, the maid would put her pads on the radiators to warm them up for her next change. I adopted this sweet, little comfort into my own self-care program from then on.

It was around this time that I noticed that if I were sitting with someone for a few minutes, listening to what they were saying, I would begin to see different faces appear in them, one after the other. I felt sure that I was seeing both their past and future visual physical incarnations, and this was confirmed a year later. I have only managed to do this with myself in the mirror very slightly and with much effort and have since learned that it could be very harmful to do this on oneself.

Denny Waxman also suggested that I try and find a local dojo where I could learn to study and practice aikido. When I got back, I looked in the phone directory but could not find any listings for dojos, so I got a copy of the local newspaper and came across an ad for somebody giving macrobiotic cooking classes and meal deliveries. I called the number and spoke with a woman called Rosemary who gave me information about a dojo in Woodstock and also kindly invited me to have lunch with her the following week, when she asked if I would like to assist her in preparation work at her cooking classes. I happily accepted, and suffice to say, we became very good friends and stayed in touch regularly right up to the last few days of her life in 2019.

I started going to aikido classes, which I found to be very interesting and enjoyed incorporating this new spiritual practice into my life. At one of Rosemary's classes, I met an interesting man named Phil who was a practicing Tibetan Buddhist. We started a relationship, and it was quite wonderful.

Phil had a kidney condition, and I suggested that he go and see Denny Waxman and that I would go with him to the consultation in New York City in order to better understand how to help him. We had a lovely day in New York City, and I was excited to start helping Phil on his healing journey. I began to stay with him quite often in his cabin in the woods near Woodstock, and once I had shown him a few new dishes, we shared meal preparations and it was a really special time.

Phil was a very good macrobiotic cook, and once again, I was filled with gratitude. He invited me to go to the Tibetan monastery nearby to take refuge, as he felt I was ready for it and that it would enhance my spiritual practice. It was a beautiful ceremony, and the Tibetan Buddhist name I was given is melodious knowledge. Sad to say, Phil was unable to maintain following the macrobiotic recommendations, ended up going on kidney dialysis, and eventually had a kidney transplant that his body rejected soon after.

We had been estranged for a year when he called me out of the blue from Albany hospital, asking me if I could pick him up and take him home to his new digs near Woodstock. He had just gone through the kidney transplant and rejection, and over the next year, I spent many weekends cooking and helping him during his recovery.

Mourka's son went to live with his dad for a while, and she decided to rent out the spare downstairs bedroom. And various interesting people, usually men, came and went over the next two years. At one point, a young friend of hers from Russia stayed in it. Igor was totally into aikido and offered to help me in practice sessions. He became curious about my macrobiotic practice and one day said, "Christina, teach me everything you know about macrobiotics."

I replied that as I was learning new things daily that it would be a very difficult job. I suggested instead that he read Denny Waxman's book *The Great Life Diet* and all he had to do was the daily body rub, half daily walk, and eat anything I offered, chewing every mouthful until it was liquid before swallowing. I then said, "See what happens next." It worked. You could say that I had him eating out of my hand. Igor began to lose some weight and to feel very healthy and grateful. He was my first macrobiotic student. I was beginning to notice more and more that this way of living and eating tends to bring out the best in people—that our essential selves begin to emerge.

Eventually, I did a trade with Mourka's landlady, doing some sewing jobs for her. In exchange, I was able to stay in either of her other little rental cottages during times when they were vacant of paying renters. It was a rather-perfect setup and gave me a chance to be with myself in my own space.

Back in the 1980s, I had purchased a rather interesting book titled *Macrobiotic Home Remedies* by Michio Kushi that included many simple and some not-so-simple, folk remedies for all kinds of ailments and conditions. I had occasion to experiment with a handful of the most simple remedies that proved time and again to work seemingly miraculous cures. Rose was a very trusting guinea pig and was grateful for the usefulness of such easy solutions for a difficult cough or desire to either delay or bring on menses.

Over the years, I have treated many bee and wasp stings and scorpion and spider bites successfully. One of the more dramatic success stories happened while I was doing some garment sewing work for Phil Void of the Dharma Bums at his Woodstock shop. One of the band members, Chris, had come upstairs to make some tea and was suddenly bitten by a bee that had found its way inside. He cried out and said he was allergic and would soon go into anaphylaxis shock if he didn't get treated ASAP. As he was dialing 911, I ran to the fridge and luckily found an old onion from which I sliced a half-moon. And while he was on the phone giving the emergency service the details, I told him I was going to rub the onion juice on the bee-sting site, and he looked skeptical but said, "Okay." After a short time, maybe a minute, he said he was actually beginning to feel better and was in a new state of shocked disbelief that I had used a regular onion to reverse what might have been a not-so-happy outcome. He had stayed on the phone during this whole time and told the 911 services that he was happy to report that he no longer needed an ambulance.

In 1994, Mourka got a new teaching job, and Rose and I needed to move to a place that was located within the New Paltz school district. During that summer, while Rose was with her dad, visiting his parents in Florida, I went back to England and surprised everyone with my new glowing health. I had put on almost forty-five pounds, and my hair was thick and long. I remember meeting my brother-in-law, Richard, in the garden, and he looked shocked and said, "Wow, Christina, what have you done that has turned things around for you in such a good way?"

I said that all I was doing was following Denny Waxman's way of life and dietary recommendations. When Rose and I rendezvoused back at Mourka's two weeks later, I found a cottage to rent fifteen minutes from her school and we moved in at the end August in time for the new school year.

Once settled, I had plenty of sewing to do for the dance company that Rose had joined and some interesting macrobiotic cooking gigs during that year. Denny Waxman called me one day, asking if he could refer me to a couple who lived in Woodstock, Elliot and

Diana. Diana had recently seen him for a consultation and needed help getting started with learning how to prepare the dishes he recommended. I asked Denny if he really thought I was healed enough to help her, and he said, "Yes, certainly."

I was truly grateful to have the opportunity at last to help someone in the way that I had been shown and felt in my element cooking and sharing in this way. I spent many days with Diana in her home on the outskirts of Woodstock and over the next three years, and we became very close. She loved the new daily practices and especially enjoyed eating in an orderly way and chewing every mouthful until it was liquid before swallowing. After our morning cooking class, we shared silent/nontalking lunches out on the deck in the warm weather or inside if cold, but both places had a beautiful view of the garden and mountains.

On my way back to Mourka's in the summer months, I would go to a special secluded pool in the river nearby and skinny-dip with the beavers. I couldn't say thank you enough to the universe for all the wondrous experiences I was being both gifted with and guided toward. There followed two more referrals over the next three years from Denny Waxman, and I really enjoyed helping these people, using Denny's recommendations, with their own condition. I also started a macrobiotic wholesale buyers' club and hosted regular potluck suppers at the cottage when friends came to pick up their orders and join in the feast.

Chapter 24

A Recurrence and a Return

However, I did suffer a bulimic recurrence during the last term that Rose was in middle school and during the Easter holidays, unable to tell her the reason, found myself needing to retreat back to the United Kingdom in order to better handle it, away from the still-new stresses of single parenting. I returned a couple of months later, back on track as Rose had always wanted to study drama and acting, and we traveled back to the United Kingdom where she spent the next four years in drama college.

MM had been wanting all her four grandchildren to each have their own flat to live in at Saint Nicholas. She really wished for us all to live there permanently, and my two sisters had settled in nicely, but I remained a part timer as my bonding to the United States was stronger than ever. The old nursery wing and the adjoining bedroom and bathroom that had been the housekeepers' home for forty-plus years became mine and Rose's flat for whenever we were there, which worked out very nicely, and I was once again most grateful to MM.

That spring of 1994, when Rose had just started her first term of college, MM (then aged ninety-three years) had just driven the cleaning help home (Margaret was eighty plus herself) in her Jaguar XJ6 and was closing the ten-foot-high, heavy, wooden garage doors that rolled around on a steel rail, when the door got stuck and she fell and broke her hip.

I just happened to have been on my way to come and see her in the house, heard her calling the familiar cook-oo, which was her way of getting attention, and found her on the ground unable to stand up. The ambulance came quickly, and she was operated on the following morning and began to make a remarkable recovery, though I am sorry to say that really was the beginning of her decline and she never drove or walked again without the aid of either crutches, a walker, or wheelchair.

I spent the next few weeks caring for her, and we became much closer. And I treasure the times we spent, especially when it was massage time or when I helped her take a little walk in the garden, which she missed being in sorely now that she was unable to tend to things herself.

I have to mention one extraordinary event that happened when I was alone with MM one afternoon. I had decided to wash all the windows in this forty-room house, which I did slowly over a two-week period. It was a typically cloudy, damp Yorkshire spring day, and I was in the downstairs back passage when I heard the front doorbell ring. MM must have been close by, for before I could get there, I heard the door being unlocked and she was speaking to someone. When I arrived by her side, to my surprise, there was a local man, John (who chose to live as a gypsy outside and who turned up periodically to ask if MM needed any odd jobs doing around the garden for cash) completely naked, except for his boots.

MM didn't bat an eye and calmly said, "John, dear, put on your clothes immediately or you will catch your death of cold. I don't need any help today, but come back next week and preferably fully clothed and I will find something for you to do." That was the last time John ever came to the house. I was very impressed by the cool way in which MM dealt with this rather-unusual situation.

During my visits to Yorkshire, I was in the habit of taking a weekly trip by foot to collect spring water from a source at the bottom edge of a wooded section of my grandmother's property, as the in-house system was fed by the treated town water. On a very cold, below-freezing midwinter's day, I walked down through the woods with my rucksack and empty plastic liter bottles, collected the water, which I loaded onto my back, and began my favorite walk home via the low path that ran alongside the river Swale.

There was some ice on both sides of the river, which was otherwise still flowing, and I was suddenly overcome with the strong feeling that I had to have a swim in this beautiful cool river. The intellectual part of me fought vigorously against this idea, saying I must be losing my mind and that I would likely die of a heart attack because it was freezing, and I just kept on walking. As the path began to veer off away from the river, the inner voice got stronger and louder, insisting on a swim, so I turned back and that was exactly what I did. There wasn't another soul about, so I stripped off and in I went, completely immersing myself in the oh-so refreshingly icy water. And it felt wonderful. Every part of my being was alive and woken up to the glory of that moment, and I was so glad that I had paid attention to what my body/spirit wanted and needed.

The walk up the hill went quicker than ever and when I arrived back at the house, immediately put on new drier clothes. And the first thing that came to mind was that I needed to have some whiskey and sardines. Sorry to say I ignored the whiskey part of the message, as I thought I shouldn't and had some warm apple juice instead. Well, I did not get a cold, but I called Denny Waxman to relate what had happened, and he said the whiskey would have been perfect and actually suggested that I have some mixed half and half with water after supper a couple of times a week while I was in Yorkshire. I reminded him of my past teenage dependency on alcohol and wondered if this was really a good idea. He said not to worry, as I had greatly changed and improved since then and explained that the whiskey would be balancing for my condition and a good warming effect against the damp, foggy, cold climate. He was right, and it really helped me to relax! Ever since then, I have got much better at listening to my inner voice for guidance.

I was able to spend more time preparing some of my favorite foods, including amazake, seitan, and sprouted Essene bread. I had once attempted to make this most delicious bread, which is a recipe passed down through the centuries originating in Eastern Europe and made using quite simply whole dehusked wheat or rye berries and water. Additional ingredients such as carrots, raisins, and seeds are optional extras. What was so special about making this chewy, sweet treat cake bread while staying with my grandmother was the fact that I used the wheat that was grown, harvested, and stored at her farm and the spring water collected by me from the source in her woodland.

Chapter 25

August 1996: Purchasing Land and Building a Cabin

I spent those years to-ing and fro-ing between Mourka's place and the United Kingdom, spending time with Rose and taking turns to help look after MM.

Just before leaving Yorkshire in May 1996, MM gifted me a generous sum for helping look after her so that I might try and find some land in the countryside with a cabin or cottage of my own to buy in Upstate New York, where she knew I now preferred and enjoyed living. She said she was envious of my freedom and that I was living a life that she wished she could have had. Even though she lived a very social life, she had always loved staying in remote, quiet places, like the ones she took us all to during tour childhood holidays. Once again, I had a better understanding of her and after all, that we had a lot more in common than I had thought. I was and am eternally grateful to her.

In July, the owner of the property where Mourka and I were living, Andre, a lovely woman in her eighties who was a veterinarian, gave us advanced notice that her eldest daughter and her family would be moving into the house she had been renting out to us that coming September. We then began the search for our new prospective homes. Initially, we thought we might go into something together, but Mourka and I had different ideas of where we wanted to be. And subsequently, she found a beautiful Victorian house in Rosendale, New York, and I eventually found the five-plus acres of raw land that is still my home base.

The way in which I found this property is an interesting story.

I had decided to incorporate the 9 Star Ki supportive directional energy into my search and taken a map of Ulster County with a 30-degree west triangle marked on it starting at Andre's property to look for a property in a westerly direction. The woman realtor who helped me only had three properties that were in my price range in her listings and that also fit inside the 30-degree west directional area. And one day in July, we set out together to go and look at them. We saw two of them of which neither really appealed to me, but we couldn't find the third one and had to give up the search for the day.

No other listings came up, and over the next few weeks, I was busy helping a friend from Paris and her young son, who were coming to live in the United States, find a place to rent. With only two weeks until we had to be out of Andre's house, even though Mourka invited me to stay with her, I decide to start looking again. I called the realtor and asked if I could go on my own to try and find the third property, to which she agreed that I could.

After driving around and around the area for about an hour, trying to decipher where I was on the map that I had, I eventually came down a private road of what was planned to become a new housing development, and that led into a cul-de-sac. I got out feeling excited that I was close to my goal and followed a little footpath going through a heavily wooded area that brought me to a clearing.

What a sight for sore eyes and all my chakras were instantly opened up. I was looking at a 180-degree view of what I later found out to be the Mombaccus Mountains, looking toward the Northwest, and I realized I had found the third property and that this was the serene and peaceful place that I seemed to have been searching for my entire life. It was an exhilarating sensation.

I went back and called the realtor immediately (no cell phones in those days) and the next day gave her a deposit, and we went and walked the land together. There was a funky but self-sufficient 1973 Volunteer trailer, which had a decal/sign on it, reading, "Happy

Little Trailer," parked facing the mountain view—which belonged to the owner (Joyce) of the back lot behind this one—and was parked there for the two property owners' summer camping use.

The trailer needed a thorough cleaning but otherwise was perfect and equipped with a two-burner propane stove with oven, a mini fridge, and a heater and was fueled by two small propane tanks that sat on a back space on the outside. Joyce said I could stay in the trailer so that I would have someplace to live until I figured out what I was going to do next. Eventually, she very kindly gifted it to me.

There was no electricity, water, or telephone, but none of that was a deterrent. I decided I would carry in water for drinking and cooking and collect rainwater off the roof of the trailer in buckets for washing purposes. There was a right-of-way access road coming in from below the land and that would be my main route driving in. The private road that I first entered by was the official address and access, but it would be several years before I would be able to afford to make a driveway onto the land from there. The next day, I decided to do my own title search over at the county offices, and two weeks later, I was the very happy owner/guardian of this beautiful piece of land.

In the afternoon of August 31, I packed up all my belongings into my car and said goodbyes to Andre and her family. Mourka had moved slowly over the previous weeks. And I went over to see her in her new home, and we ate supper. I then drove over to my land in an amazing end-of-summer, thunder-and-lightning storm with rain coming down in sheets.

The first thing I did was to put an empty bucket under the corner of the trailer to collect rainwater for washing needs and simply unloaded a few things from the car to make enough room in the back seat so that I could sleep on the folded futon and bedding there for the night. I cleaned the stove top, boiled some of the rainwater for my evening body rub, dashed back to the car in the still-torrential rain, and was asleep instantly.

In the morning, I awoke feeling so filled with grace and gratitude and the sound of the birds on a magical sunny day. I boiled some rainwater in the trailer to do my a.m. body rub; put breakfast on to cook; did some slow, luxurious yoga; and then walked around the front path with the sun shining on the dewy, sparkling raindrop, jewel-laden cobwebs, wild rose, blackberry bushes, and trees. It was another one of the most extraordinary days of my life, and I was filled with great gratitude and love for all with that I was newly blessed.

I ate breakfast sitting outside and afterward while I was washing up, began to hear some heavenly flute music coming from the access road below and decided to try and find the source of this gift. Walking down the same road I had driven up the night before, I followed the music until I came upon a man sitting outside his cabin, playing what turned out to be a handmade traditional Native American flute. He had a gentle-looking, long-haired golden retriever sitting by his side.

I introduced myself as a new neighbor and owner of the land above, and the man, Tom, was totally welcoming and said that he had spent time with Native Americans who had shown him how to find the wood to carve a flute and taught him to play it. He said he had been playing music on my land for several years because the spirits of the native ancestors had guided him there.

I felt so lucky to be serenaded in such a way on my first morning. Tom insisted that I come and fill up my drinking water bottles with water from his well, and as there was an outside tap, he said I could come down anytime whether he was home or not. He also offered that I could come and have a hot shower when needed—a truly wonderful neighbor.

I set off to go back up the road and realized that the dog, Sadie, had followed me home. She went straight underneath the trailer and settled down as though this was her usual routine. I did a little cleaning and got the car unpacked and a little later, walked her back down to Tom. He explained that she and his neighbors' dogs were free to roam around outside in the daytime and had not ever caused any problems, and he was glad if she came to keep me company if I didn't mind.

So Sadie became my new daytime, under-the-trailer housemate and friend, appearing walking up the access road in the mornings around 8:00 a.m. after Tom had left for work and then simply getting up and leaving at 5:00 p.m. when she knew he was coming home. I loved that dog and the way she guarded me. And every time I came out of the trailer to go for a walk, she would come with me, and when I left to drive somewhere, she was there when I came back as long as it was before 5:00 p.m. I never fed her a single morsel of food because that wasn't the nature of our relationship, and she wasn't, after all, my dog nor did I wish to own her. Once in a while, the other dogs would all appear, chasing a rabbit or just going on a walkabout, and sometimes Sadie joined in and sometimes she just watched them go by.

The peace and quiet of my new home was unsurpassable, and the fact that I owned it meant that I had a degree of privacy and solitude that I had so longed for in my life and until this point in time, had never achieved. I spent the next two weeks there, going nowhere and speaking only with my new neighbor, Tom, on that first day.

Later on, looking back, it was perhaps a rather a selfish act because friends and family were worried about me when I next saw or spoke with them. But I truly had all that I needed to stay there comfortably during that time, and I did not ever once feel alone, afraid, unhappy, or lacking in any way. I was able to eat all my meals on time in a whole new level of relaxation without any interruption or stresses of phones ringing, fridges humming, people coming in and out, or dogs barking.

I discovered anew the great and wonderful gift of not having any need to talk, and this was my initiation into my now-preferred practice of being in silence more often than not. Out of this practice has been born an ability to listen, hear, and feel all the messages of nature, internally and externally, without interference. I often get strong insights and/or messages while walking alone quietly in the woods or while doing yoga and especially when I am eating in silence.

I realized that my sensitive nature and nervous system craved this level of peace and quiet, and my entire being began to truly relax in ways that I had never before experienced. I wandered around my property and explored the surrounding heavily wooded acres that made up approximately eighty acres of this land development divided into fifteen of which my five acres was one lot. Only one other lot had been sold, and the owner was using it as a storage place.

Telephone poles were in place, but no electricity currents ran along them, and it felt very calming to my central nervous system.

On the second day, I came across two coyotes crossing over the official driveway in and they looked at me for a moment and as quick as lightning, disappeared into the woods. A gift indeed.

I thoroughly cleaned and organized the Happy Little Trailer, and everything worked fine, though I had yet to try and light the propane heater and made some minor repairs to windows and drawers. There had obviously been a lot of mice in residence and probably still were, but they didn't bother me until they began getting into things and making nests with lots of babies. And I had to carry the nests outside and start trapping the frantic parents in a have-a-heart trap and walking them way off into the woods before setting them free. (Once the cabin was built, I am sorry to say they eventually began to take over the place and more drastic methods have had to be used ever since.)

My days flowed, and I was the most content I had ever been in my life to that point. My personal daily rituals and macrobiotic practice served me so well with super-bright, strong energy, and I was so very grateful for being so blessed.

In the evenings, I lit candles and read, wrote letters, played solitaire, or sewed. I did my body rub and happily got into bed with the sounds of owls and coyotes to send me into deep, peaceful sleep.

I noticed that when it rained heavily, there were seasonal streams flowing in many places, and the large area of rock face at the top of the property, adjacent to the trailer on the right side facing the mountains, had a natural pond formation that collected a large amount of water. However, it drained out over a few days, and I decided that at some point, I would chink it with some clay in order to prevent the water from seeping underground and hopefully create a natural habitat for the frogs that seemed to be around.

After two weeks, it was time to go back out into the world, stock up on supplies, and let everyone know I was alive and indeed very well and happy. I went to the local health food coop and immediately was asked by the managers if I would consider to help do the catering for the coop semiannual harvest party as a paid job plus get lifetime membership at the coop. This was a great gift gig. I was honored to be asked and had so much fun preparing some of my favorite delicious macrobiotic vegan dishes for the event, which was a great success.

This was the beginning of a new phase in my macrobiotic cooking career.

Chapter 26

Starting a Community Barter System and Practicing a More Sustainable Lifestyle

On the last trip back to the United Kingdom, I had attended some interesting meetings with a good friend of Mum's. LETS is a local exchange and trade community barter system that has been operating successfully in Canada, United Kingdom, and Australia for many years. The barter system intrigued me, and I felt that it had a strong place in my life. So when I mentioned it to a friend at the coop, he got very excited and said he knew some good people who would be very open to helping start a community barter system in Ulster County.

A meeting was set up at the Stone Ridge Cultural Co-Op Community one evening in early October. It was an instant success, and Ulster County LETS was born. Our currency was to be wampum (which was changed a few years later to acorns), but the system would run on the same credit/debit format of the LETS in the United Kingdom, so no actual money had to be printed. Various local businesses were mentioned as very likely and possible new members, and my vision of the barter system was very strong and clear.

During that meeting, everyone said what services they could share and when they heard about my new property, said that they would like to help me build a cabin in exchange for some macrobiotic meals and sewing jobs. It was perfect. I should mention that at this point in my life, having put every penny into buying the property and not wishing to have to pay a monthly fee just to keep a checking account, I chose to close my bank account. It seemed like the perfect opportunity to see if I could live in a different, more sustainable way. I was living from day to day on whatever cash I earned from various cooking and housekeeping and assistant gigs that I managed to juggle. I had not had a credit card since separating from Ben, and I liked it that way. I felt very free and light.

A few days later, Charlie, Paul, and Sam showed up on my land to assess the situation, and they drew up a simple plan for a structure to be built over the trailer that would then be closed in for that first winter. Then in the springtime, the trailer would be pulled out and the cabin could then be completed. We walked around the property and marked eighteen nice, straight, young hickory trees that would be needed for the main structural posts and beams.

The following week, they returned with saws, hammers, and a huge metal bucket of old/bent nails (which I spent hours flattening out on a large flat stone with a hammer) and chopped down the hickory trees we had marked. These trees were then placed on large flat stones gathered from the property and then the frame was all nailed together and secured with crosspieces. It just so happened Charlie was a master carpenter who had just finished building a beautiful post-and-beam house and a straw-bale cabin. Paul was also a most capable builder/didgeridoo maker/player and jack-of-all-trades, and Sam had knowledge and access to many building materials and tools, so I felt completely surrounded by very capable builders.

Because I had spent every single penny that I had to buy this property, it became obvious that we should use all available resources possible. Recycled materials began to be collected and donated. The local recycling transfer station had a great system in that people could bring unwanted materials and appliances and anyone could take them. It was amazing how much people discarded and nearly all the windows, doors, and screens came from there.

Sam, who was running the Stoneridge Cultural Co-Op, donated a load of sturdy, old lumber; some doors; useful tools; and ladders to the project. They suggested that a woodstove could be put in the area outside the trailer, the heat of which would suffice to keep me toasty for the coming winter months. Additionally, Charlie knew the local town building codes and said that if the structure were kept a certain size, we would not need to obtain a permit. He was right.

It all happened so smoothly and quickly, and at the end of the first day, a beautiful, natural sixteen-foot-by-eighteen-foot wooden structure surrounded the trailer on all sides. I fed everyone rice, garbanzo bean stew, and blanched salad and was so very grateful and happy to be alive.

It was decided that in order to make the whole structure waterproof that we should buy all new roofing materials and so I borrowed $180 to go with Paul to buy the plywood, roll roofing, and nails. Sam donated a roll of tar paper that had been sitting unused for a year. That was the total amount of dollars that was spent on the initial structure.

On a sunny cold day in November, I was up on the top of a ladder—held by Sam—that was leaning against the frame and was holding the pieces of plywood, while Paul hammered in the nails and made me laugh so hard, I thought I would fall off. The view up there was spectacular, and it was so exhilarating to be helping in the building of my new home.

Sam also donated six-by-eight gallon water containers with screw tops so that I had a way to bring in my potable/drinking water. I picked up all the empty, five-gallon, bulk nut butter and tahini containers from the High Falls Food Co-op, and they became my rainwater-collecting buckets and later on the outhouse collectors.

My new building contractor friends endearingly nicknamed the cabin the Taj Mahal of Tabasco, as it was starting to look a lot bigger and grander than any of us had imagined it would.

One sunny afternoon, when I was walking the property, I came across a very large black snake that rattled its warning and I got the message loud and clear to back away. I found out a few days later that it was a timber rattlesnake, which were quite commonly found in the area back then but now are less often seen since all the new houses have been built.

Toward the end of October that year, there was a total eclipse of the moon. We had built a small firepit on a flat area of the rock face, and that night, I lit a fire and sat, watching the eclipse with awe and gratitude for the amazing, unobstructed night sky view that my land offered.

Early in December, a big snowstorm arrived and that was the beginning of what turned out to be a very severe, long, cold, snowy winter. It put an end to the building plan, which was postponed until the spring. I had to abandon my trailer, ended up going to spend the next few months in the Stone Ridge Cultural Co-op, and in lieu of rent, served macrobiotic food in the open kitchen café.

I returned to my land just after a late April snowstorm and began anew the building projects. What was quite amazing was that I had left three large fruit farm boxes with my glass storage jars under the cabin covered with a heavy slab of wood. And when I returned, the top two had been pushed aside with nothing broken and only one of the jars in the bottom box had been taken out somehow and broken. It was natural brown sugar that I had kept from earlier pre-macrobiotic days. A bear had intuited that it was the only thing he wanted.

The only other times bears have interfered with anything were when I had a solar shower bag heating up on the natural rock slab whilst I was out delivering food for the day, and when I came home, it was burst from a bear's claws penetrating the plastic/rubber bag. The outhouse also once was completely pushed over, which cracked but did not actually smash the only glass window in it. And a few times, the heavy compost bin was pushed over. Nowadays, it is secured to the sturdy pine tree that it sits against.

Chapter 27

1997: Outhouse and Tent Platform

Soon after I moved back to my trailer, Mourka introduced me to a young man she had recently met called George who was a carpenter visiting from South Carolina. He was a delightfully respectful Southerner with a great deal of charm and good manners. He got an apprentice job at a local carpenters' workshop, and his grandmother gifted him birthday money to buy a super tent in which to live. He set the tent up on my land and began to help with the various building projects.

He brought back plenty of salvaged wood from his workplace and built a sturdy platform for his super tent. He was also part of a men's group that met once a month, and he organized for the twelve men in his group to come over on the twelfth day of the month at noon to help finish the cabin roof and build the outhouse.

I fed them all, and it was an extraordinary day of like-minded, caring people all pulling together to help in the project. Unfortunately, two things happened simultaneously: George's beautiful tent was not sturdy enough to withstand a very strong windy storm that blew in one afternoon, and it broke the main stays. And then a few days later, he had an accident at his workplace and almost severed his fingers while using a Skilsaw. He was unable to use his hand for many weeks in order to let it heal and so he ended going back home to South Carolina. George had really enjoyed the food I offered him. And during the following two summers, he stopped by to visit me and see

112

how things were progressing, and it just so happened that on the days he came by, I had made millet with sweet vegetable porridge, which was his favorite dish.

Soon after George left, I put an advertisement in the classified section of the *Woodstock Times* offering a barter situation for anyone wanting a place to live. They could pitch a tent and I would feed them simply delicious macrobiotic food, and in exchange, they would be asked to help finish the cabin.

During this time, I continued cooking and delivering macrobiotic meals on wheels for Diana, Charlie and his son, and a neighbor who lived in an old, converted firehouse and was dealing with cancer.

Three times a week, I prepared three course meals in my little trailer for six people, including myself, with enough for a second serving, all cooked on the two-burner trailer gas stove top. And looking back, I simply don't know how I pulled it off.

Chapter 28

1997: Mummy and Winnie Visit the Homestead

My mother came over from England in June with her traveling companion and dear family friend, Winnie, in time to celebrate my fortieth birthday. They stayed at an inn in Woodstock, and I picked them up each day after I had done any cooking that I had committed to doing. One day, I brought them back to the land and we ate lunch on the rock next to the cabin frame. Mum called it my hut and it has a been an endearing joke ever since. I was still cooking, delivering food, and helping Diana, and I took Mum and Winnie to meet her. Later on, Mum treated me; Winnie; Mourka; her future husband, Miklos; and Igor and his girlfriend to a birthday supper at the Japanese restaurant in Rhinecliff. It was a beautiful summer's day full of love and gratitude. After a few days, I put Mum and Winnie back on the Amtrak train heading up to Niagara Falls on the next leg of their holiday tour of the Northeast United States and Canada.

Not long after they left, I had a most extraordinary experience/vision/dream. To this day, I cannot say for sure what to call it, for it was as real as anything I normally experience.

It was very early in the morning when I was awakened by what seemed to be a car light coming up the right-of-way driveway and was sending its beam of light straight into the trailer. I sat up and watched the light coming closer to the trailer and then realized that it wasn't a car, as the light was the most amazing, brilliant blue and I couldn't see or tell what was creating this light, as it was so bright. I got up, stood at the screen door of the trailer looking out, slowly opened the door, and stepped down onto the trailer step-up, just as the blue light went right through me from left to right in a steady motion. And I was, simply put, filled up with this beautiful light. And just as soon as it had come, it was gone. And in awe, I went back to lie down so that I could just process the energy that seemed to have flooded my whole being and was causing me to feel so incredibly happy, grateful, and full of love for all. The blue light stayed with me for many weeks afterward, and even now, twenty-two years later, when I think of it, I am filled with that wonder and awe.

That summer, I was being visited by a gray female cat who started to have a big belly of kittens. I had not ever fed any of the stray animals and made sure that the kitchen scraps were under a heavy-lidded composting area so as not to make any kind of dependency imbalance. It was always touching that I got these visits. I went away for a few weeks, and when I came back, the cat came to see me, minus her big belly. I kept asking her, "Where are your babies, Mama?" And then after about a week, she brought them up to visit me, one by one in her mouth, all four of them. Presumably, they all moved on, as after a while, the visits stopped.

The cabin project was chugging along at a slow but steady pace, and materials that were needed for any part of the building—be it siding, flooring, insulation—all miraculously appeared.

No cement or concrete was used, and instead, we used pressure-treated floor rafters, then recycled floor planking, tar paper on top, and then donated/found plywood subfloor. The second layer of plywood flooring had a large irregular gap. And one day, I was driving home from doing some house organizing for a friend and noticed a large piece of irregular-shaped plywood on the side of the road next to trash cans with a free sign on it, except for one small cut that needed to be made. That piece of plywood plopped right into the cabin subfloor, like the missing piece of an intricate jigsaw puzzle. Amazing universal synchronicity.

The main floor eventually appeared three years later and was donated and dropped off by one of the LETS barter system members, Will. It consisted of three large, plastic milk crates of twelve-inch-by-three-inch, tongue-in-groove oak parquet floor boards that he had carefully taken out of a church that had burned down back in Wisconsin in 1978 and he had stored in the basement of his home in Ulster County ever since. Tom lent me a nail-flooring tool, and the parquet floor was laboriously put down in 2002.

Chapter 29

Winter Quarters

It was clear that trying to stay the winter on my land in the Happy Little Trailer was not a sensible option so. Once again, with the help of the 9 Star Ki directional suggestions, I chose a southeast location and was gratefully hosted to stay with the dear friends and godparents of Rose, Bob and Lois, who lived (and still do) in a lovely, old house they bought in Glen Cove, Long Island, New York.

I took all my kitchen supplies, had a lovely room and bathroom to myself, and was in relative luxury for the entire winter. I always make sure that there is a gas stove for cooking on before I stay with anyone and if not, will either bring my own portable butane stoves that I use for teaching situations. Luckily, I already knew that there was indeed a lovely, big, commercial-style gas stove at the Glen Cove house. Bob and Lois owned a French café and made large quantities of fresh soup for their patrons on that stove. I ate all my meals quietly alone mainly because Bob and Lois at the time were not particularly attracted to my way of eating and we also had different mealtimes. It was very nurturing to be with friends for the coldest winter months, and during those months, I was inspired to create a business pamphlet that I intended to put in strategic places when I returned upstate. This is what the voice within helped me to write:

Within each of us exists all the information of the entire universe. But we have either forgotten it and/or it is blocked or stuck deep within our DNA cells due to all the generational afore years of inappropriate diets and lifestyles that took us further and further away from our most natural and divine source of knowledge and knowing.

Toward the end of April 1998, when spring was in full bloom in Glen Cove, I was ready and happy to make the return journey to my land, again with the help of the 9 Star Ki system. I did, however, underestimate the weather and all that I would need to do once I got back up there, and it felt at one point that I had severely stressed my system. From that point on, I found that I needed to pace myself much more carefully and still do to this day.

Chapter 30

Caring for MM and a Relapse

Two days after I arrived back, I got a call from Mum saying that MM had a minor heart attack and the doctor said that she might only have a few days or weeks left to live. I immediately booked a ticket and flew back to the United Kingdom to be there with her. After days of family and friends coming and going to pay their respects and we were alone together as I massaged her feet, she confided, "Teeny, I live for the times you massage my feet and I have no intention of dying yet. I wish everyone would just go away and leave me/us in peace." She lived another two years.

As my apartment was now being used by the caregivers who were living in whilst caring for MM, I stayed with Mum during the visit. I was challenged on many levels and especially to maintain my regular daily rituals and mealtimes. It was hard to adjust to the new time zone, and on the third morning as I was trying to relax to have a very late (by the United Kingdom time zone) breakfast, the front door bell rang. And Mum's dog started barking, and my whole body went into a place of shock. I can only describe it as feeling that an icy cold metal liquid raced around my whole torso, starting in the base of my spine and going up and around in a circle several times. A voice within said, "Your food eating disorder has returned," and my heart rate had greatly accelerated.

It was a very frightening experience that I shared with no one, and I am not sure how I got through the next few days, but I had a hard time relaxing to eat and felt cold and afraid. I remember taking a hot bath one night that seemed to relax me in the moment and actually noticing how lovely and full my body looked and felt. However, from that point on, I must have steadily lost a lot of weight, as eating normally/enough seemed to elude me.

Somehow, I managed to get back to the United States and up to my land and then all hell broke loose in my system, and I thought there was indeed a problem with my heart. My beautiful, new, thick, lustrous hair was falling out in great handfuls. And any small, natural exertion seemed life-threatening. I went to get tests done, which included wearing a Holter monitor for several days. The results showed only that my heart rate was indeed much faster than normal but not in a dangerous way.

I managed to get a consultation to see Denny Waxman because I simply couldn't figure out what was happening in my system and he wasn't immediately able to figure it out until I went back to have a second consult when, after telling a few more details of what I was experiencing, he realized that all my organs had systematically contracted when I got shocked. He said it had happened because my diet had been too yang and narrow and he recommended a radical change to help the condition. This included adding in 50 percent non-macrobiotic foods to my daily fare and especially using cream, butter, milk, caffeine, chocolate, and sugar.

I need to mention here that something very interesting happened on this second visit with Denny. Just before I was about to walk into his consulting room, the door had just been opened, and when I looked up, I saw in the armchair at the back of the room a very large, brown, velvet being. And I sensed that it was the energy being of Denny Waxman, who soon after materialized / came into focus in place of the velvet being. I have not ever told him about this.

So after the consultation, I set off to try and start to put his recommendations into practice. At first, I was hopeful and excited, but after trying some coffee and pancakes with syrup, I became very confused and upset by these new foods because I had become so used to eating simply delicious, calming energy foods for the past nine years.

I also had many days when I felt depressed and thought of past difficulties and dying, which seemed so strange after the past eleven years of feeling constantly grateful and excited to be alive. It was a very confusing and scary time, and I even experimented taking half low-dose Valium, which helped get me through a few especially difficult times. I also tried an antidepressant, but that really upset my spiritual balance.

When I shared all of this with Denny, he said it was part of the contracted condition, and he was the first person whom I had ever heard suggest that actually allowing myself to feel and go through a depressed state was a more beneficial practice than attempting to avoid it. In all the years I have sought his consul and attended his lectures and workshops, Denny has rarely given support to taking any medications or vitamin supplements other than B12, which is often lacking in the vegetarian/macro diet. It was yet another confirmation of the idea that using a carefully guided macrobiotic approach to health and healing could help to draw out old energy from the past that becomes lodged deep inside the cells.

Denny also suggested that I stop doing any yoga or disciplinary activity for a while, except for the daily body rub and half-hour walk. He said that it might take six months to ease myself out of this energy-contracted upset. I realized that by applying his recommendations, I was helping, once again, to relax my thinking, which was seeing things from the contracted condition of my organs. Unlike the first time I saw him—when his suggestions were all mildly sweet-tasting, gentle, calming, macrobiotic, quality dishes/food that soothed my system and especially spoke to my spirit—this time, a more extreme method was needed. I am happy to say that it worked, although it actually took more than a year.

It was necessary to find an alternative place to stay while I concentrated on once again healing myself, and using the 9 Star Ki system for the most supportive direction, I moved into a little cottage about twenty minutes away from my land down in the valley. During that year, I did manage to go to England for one of Rose's performances at the drama college she attended. I also was able to help a dear friend who had breast cancer learn to cook the dishes that

Denny was recommending, and I actually lived in her house for a few weeks before making the trip back up the mountain to my land.

It was good to be home again, and I was also feeling much more relaxed thanks to my very relaxing way of eating.

Chapter 31

Back on the Land

There was much to do back on the land, and various cabin projects were continued during that summer, particularly getting more rough-cut siding onto the sides of the cabin.

I started a couple of new cooking jobs, helping two dear friends: one with cancer, who was under Denny's guidance, and the other, an interesting woman who taught Kabbalah sound healing. One day, I had just delivered food to them both, and on my way home, a baby deer jumped in front of the car and was seriously injured.

Fortunately, Charlie just happened to drive by and he kindly helped me to take the fawn out of her misery. She did not die immediately, and it was a shocking and heartbreaking event.

Afterward, we put the fawn into the back of my station wagon, and Charlie said he had some Russian friends whom he felt would be grateful of the animal, as they, in a traditional respectful way, would use all the parts.

We planned to meet at the coop after he got the go-ahead from his friends. While I was waiting for Charlie, a local Native American woman I knew from the LETS happened to be there. And when I told her the sad story, she said that traditionally, after a wild animal has been killed, the one who has done the killing would eat the cooked heart. However, if the animal suffered during its slaying, its heart should be buried in a special place in nature with a ceremony of lighted candle and prayers.

Charlie took the fawn to his friends so that they could begin the skinning process, and I went back to the trailer for a tearful supper and afterward, joined them to help strip the meat off the sinew/muscle, which would be dried/cured and used as strings in the bow the family used for hunting. When the whole process was completed, I joined them at their supper table in prayers of gratitude (and forgiveness) and toasted the spirit of the fawn with a shot of vodka and I also ate a small piece of the freshly cooked venison in respect of the life I had taken. I was given the uncooked heart to take home with me. And the following day, I went into the woods on my land, lit a candle, said prayers, and then buried it there. It was a very sad and difficult experience, and I grieved for the loss of this sweet creature for several weeks afterward. The following year, a mother deer and her two fawns ran across my path and went directly over the heart burial place. It seemed like a good sign.

Chapter 32

Hawaii 2000 and Grandmother's Death

One day in August, I got a call from my dear friend, Rosemary, whom I had met in Woodstock back in 1993, inviting me to go to Maui, Hawaii, to cook for her for two weeks. Initially, I hesitated, but a friend urged to me go, saying it would be the most wonderful experience. So on September 4 early in the morning, I set off from the trailer to travel to Maui. It was an almost-cloudless, sunny, daytime flight going across the entire United States. The window seat afforded me a view that took my breath away and opened me up in another whole new way.

I wrote down my feelings and simply described the extraordinary scenes below that were constantly changing before my eyes. Rosemary met me at the airport, and I was so happy and grateful to her for inviting me to be there, as it is truly a magical place. The two weeks stretched out into almost three months. Another dear woman friend, Nancy, and her family, who had moved from Upstate New York in the eighties, invited me to live in and help with child minding while she was at work. I also did several house-sitting gigs for some of her friends and made macrobiotic meals a few times a week for Rosemary's friends when she was traveling for a few weeks.

Late in October, I went to stay with a dear, new Maui friend called Irene in her B and B on the coast in a very remote and special place on the island called Hana. On the night of October 28, while I was painting her toenails and telling her how I did this for my grandmother, the phone call came in from my mother saying that MM had died.

Mum also said that the night before when she went in to say goodnight, MM had said that she had had a wonderful life and that she was ready to leave. She died peacefully in her sleep five months shy of her one hundredth birthday in the bed that had been custom made for her and my grandfather in 1922.

I booked a flight and the next day traveled from Hawaii to New York and then onto the United Kingdom for the funeral of MM, which was held in Saint Mary's Church in Richmond, North Yorkshire—the same church where we had all attended Sunday services and Sunday school all through our childhood. It was a very big and beautiful service, and tears of love and gratitude flowed in abundance.

Sadly, the reality was that there were some debts that needed attention and so the cleaning and packing up of the place that had been home had to be started immediately. And it was put on the market to be sold soon after.

Chapter 33

Back Home

I returned to the United States and secured a couple of house-sitting gigs near Woodstock, New York, during the winter months and eventually bought an old Buick Sedan, which enabled me to start doing some cooking jobs again. In the spring of 2001, I went back to my property and with help from a dear friend, was able to finish putting the siding windows and doors on the cabin.

MM had gifted all her family portions of her estate years before she died, and in late July, my siblings and I each got a quarter portion from the sale of the house in Yorkshire.

With my share, I was able to have a well dug/pounded and bought a hand-operated simple pump. I also bought a propane fridge, cooking stove, on-demand hot water heater, woodstove, kitchen sink, and very small starter solar system in order to have some off-the-grid electricity.

A wonderful eco-landscaping crew came over and helped to clean out the natural pond area, and we chinked it with clay and straw (wattle and daub as it's called in England) in an effort to hold the rainwater in longer from seeping through the rock crevice. And for a while, after a really heavy rain, I was able to swim two full breast strokes. It has since been redone and chinked with a nontoxic concrete/cement and has been completely taken over by beautiful, tall pond grasses, newts, frogs, and lots of algae.

That summer, my daughter returned to the United States of America to work for her uncle's company in New York City and came to stay with me for the first time now that I actually had a place for her to stay. We put a mosquito net over the bed, as there still were no screens in many of the windows, and she christened the newly completed cabin by spending the first night there. It was a very special occasion. She also requested to do yoga with me in the mornings, as she had a strong feeling that she wanted to study yoga. Who would have thought that twenty-three years after I had begun my own practice and was in the habit of keeping my baby daughter close by me at all times that she would suddenly know that it was her vocation?

We had the first inside-the-cabin wildlife moment when a garter snake appeared above the bed one morning. We coaxed it outside without too much trouble, as they are after all very shy creatures and prefer to be away from humans. There have been several more snake incidents over the years, and I have come to accept them as being part of my cabin life.

My daughter's boyfriend joined us there from the United Kingdom, and he helped build the loft above the bed area for which I am still always grateful.

Over the course of the next year, several wonderful friends, both separate from and within the community barter system, appeared to help with the installations of appliances, woodstove, and kitchen sink. I bought an empty wine barrel from a local winery in order to catch the rainwater off the cabin roof, and Tom M built a platform for it above the newly installed propane tanks and ran the waterlines to hook up to the only faucet in the sink. The water that came out of the tap had a strong Bordeaux smell for many years to come and was the source of many a joke with visitors. Many hours of hard work, interesting conversations, shared macrobiotic meals, and much fun and laughter later, the cabin was beginning to be a self-reliant home.

I planned out the interior of the cabin with the help of the feng shui map that I had made using the information that I had gathered at a feng shui workshop Denny Waxman held that I had attended a few years earlier. For the first time in many years, I was able to help design, build, and set up my kitchen in the simple, practical, and natural orderly way that I had come to enjoy. And being such a small space made it quite easy and fun to do. Everything is easily accessed and within reach. This saves time, which, as I spend a fair amount of almost every day cooking, is an important ingredient. It's an open-plan, L-shaped area, which Tom S built for me. All the grains and beans are in glass quart mason jars with sealable lids and arranged on open wooden shelves to the right side of my workspace area and facing the sink.

There is a large window in front of the workspace counter looking out into the woods behind, and the morning sun comes shining in on all that I do there. Large cooking pots and pans have their home on the window shelf next to the eating table, and the rest are kept in the oven compartment of the stove, as I rarely do any baking and it's a handy, space-saving place for them. All other items are in mouse-proof containers on the large shelves under the countertop. Homemade curtains are the doors. The gas stove is at the far-left side of the counter, and all wooden cooking utensils are in a ceramic container at the right side of it with the stainless steel ones all hanging on hooks from the lip of the shelves above it. Stainless steel and ceramic containers for cooked food and other travel containers are on those shelves above the stove. The large, white, enameled kitchen sink is in front of a large window so that when washing up, I can look out into nature.

While building and organizing the interior of the cabin, mimicking nature as closely as possible has been the main goal all along. To this day, there isn't a day goes by that I don't look around the cabin with a smile and say thank-you for the sweetness of the place. It continues to be a work in progress as I become more enlightened and am inspired to make new improvements.

Chapter 34

Move to Hawaii via West Turn, 2001

On the morning of September 11, 2001, I woke up in the Happy Little Trailer feeling well rested and peaceful as was my custom. After putting on some millet with sweet kabocha squash for porridge and doing my morning rituals, I ate breakfast. Then a dear friend, Andi, who was camping on the property as a work exchange, arrived for his breakfast, and we chatted about the days' projects.

I then turned on the telephone and started to wash up. Within five minutes, the phone rang. And Tom, who had been up helping with some building work the day before, said that he was staring in disbelief at the television screen as the Twin Towers in New York City collapsed due to two American Airlines purposefully crashing into them.

I immediately called Rose, who had seen some of it, had been sent home from her workplace along with most of New York City, and was walking home toward Brooklyn as the city was gridlocked. The day before, just as Tom was leaving, we had both commented that there were so many planes flying over the property, going between the northern New York state airport. That was the last time I would see a plane overhead for several days, as all flights were canceled, including the one that I was booked on with United Airlines that was due to leave Thursday the fourteenth bound for San Francisco.

That was to be the first leg of a round-the-world west turn that I had planned a few weeks earlier with the help and guidance of

Denny using the 9 Star Ki cosmology system. This trip would help me gather strong energy in love, life, and work areas. As soon as I returned, I would need to make a decision about where I wanted to live and work and really try and settle my energy.

Being the naturally strong-willed and determined person that I am, I decided that I needed to get myself booked on a bus straight away in order to get to San Francisco in time to catch the booked flight to Hong Kong. And that was exactly what I did. I carefully packed up all the prepared food and snacks I needed for the journey and spent the next three days on a Greyhound bus along with a fairly full bus of some interesting people.

I should mention that I have found that certain foods, along with as much variety as possible, seem to work best for me when I travel. I usually take a couple of different bean dishes, nshima, kinpira, a variety of grains, including cooked millet with sweet veggies, rice/barley, porridge, and variety of lightly cooked and salad vegetable dishes.

Some of the food had started to go a bit sour, and by the time we got to Salt Lake City, Utah, I was really ready for something hot and had a very delicious creamy mushroom soup from the bus station restaurant. I managed to keep practicing all my daily rituals, except doing any yoga that required lying down. I ate all my meals on time and did the body rub whenever the bus stopped for maintenance and driver changeover.

At the first stop in Albany, I got to watch the video of the planes crashing into the Twin Towers and some of the aftermath. It really was very shocking, though it seems that I had been spared having any visual of the event prior to this for which I was grateful, as I might not have been so determined to follow through with the trip.

One thing that stood out on the journey was the feeling or reverence that all my fellow passengers seemed to emanate. A young couple and a single man had been down near the Twin Towers when the planes hit them, and they had been covered in ash as they tried to flee the area. They were in a state of shock and also gratitude for their lives being spared. There was also a Native American woman in her sixties who was traveling with her beautiful, six-month-old baby boy back to her home in Sacramento, California. Her story was interesting in that she had been going through menopause when she got pregnant with her ninth baby. She had a normal delivery and had just been to visit her father in Rochester, New York. My maternal side emerged, and along with another young couple, we took turns holding and amusing the baby so that his Mum could get some rest. The baby was a joy to behold. He looked like a baby Buddha and never stopped smiling and being happy the entire three days of travel.

We arrived in the early morning, and I had the whole day and one night in San Francisco. I explored the neighborhood around the YMCA hostel where I stayed and took the tram to get some bodywork with a shiatsu practitioner that had been recommended to me by a friend in New York. I still had a some of my own food and supplemented it with a veggie burger for supper and some hot oatmeal in the morning for breakfast from the YMCA café.

The flight to Hong Kong was an overnight and very crowded flight. It seems China Airlines permits all sorts of interesting items in the cabins, and the seats are so close together, there is barely room for anyone with longer legs. It was a rather long and cozy trip to say the least, and I was thankful when we landed safely twelve hours later.

The airport on Lantau Island is immaculate as are all the trains that ferry passengers to and from Hong Kong Island. You could eat off the floors, which were shining and spotless and no rubbish anywhere to be seen. A refreshing experience. My hotel was almost at the top of the volcano mountain on which much of the city is built. My room was on the twenty-second floor with non-opening windows but with a view to behold indeed. One of the first things I did was to have a shower and order some breakfast of oatmeal, broccoli, and a poached egg.

Then I set off to explore Hong Kong. Originally, there were only sets of stairways for pedestrians to use to go down to the very steep hill to the markets and shops and then everyone would need to carry their shopping back up all the steps. Luckily for me, escalators were installed in 1993 and have all since been refurbished. It's the longest outdoor-covered escalator system in the world, spanning 443 feet from top to bottom. I noticed, however, that there were a number of elderly women who were bypassing the luxury of the moving stairway and walking up the steps with their heavy bags laden with the day's groceries. I doubted that I would be joining them on my return later.

I remember going into a clothing shop and overhearing the two young women shopkeepers talking about the feng shui of the day. It was very refreshing, knowing that children are taught basic, important, spiritually life-supporting systems that serve them throughout their lives. I had also learned from Sue H in Yorkshire, United Kingdom, with whom I studied tai chi that in China, young children must practice the art of tai chi, walking for two years before anything else is taught.

It had been highly recommended by a friend that I try and find a good noodle shop during my stay in Hong Kong so as lunchtime approached, I began to keep my eyes open for one. Lo and behold, almost immediately, I was attracted to one where I was able to see the cook stirring the broth that he was creating, and the aromas were very appealing. I asked for the house bowl of noodles and broth and after doing my prayers to settle to eat, began to eat.

What a great experience, as every mouthful tasted like nectar. When I had finished, the waiter, who had apparently noticed my slow, careful pace and way of eating (my eyes tend to close often while chewing), approached with two small new bowls of side dishes for me to sample—tofu cooked in a delicious sauce with seaweed and shrimp in another very different sauce. He brought about four more dishes for me to try, and I can only describe it as heavenly food. The bill hardly reflected all that I had been given and offered, and I was smiling inside and out as I thanked him profusely for such a great culinary experience and went off on my merry way.

Later on, I picked up some takeout food from a Cantonese restaurant and went back to the hotel. There was an infinity pool on the sixteenth floor, and that was another extraordinary experience—swimming toward the endless edge with the whole of Hong Kong City with the mountains of mainland China in the background as the view. It was about 88 degrees Fahrenheit for most of the five days that I was there, so the pool became an almost-daily way to cool down and be refreshed.

It had also been suggested that I try and get some bodywork whilst in Hong Kong, and the concierge of the hotel highly recommended the Blind School of Massage, where students have to practice on people in order to become qualified. I was given the address, which I easily found down the hill and managed to get an appointment almost immediately with a blind woman, who was led into the room by a colleague, who also interpreted for us, as I answered questions asked of me by the masseuse.

Only women are allowed to give bodywork treatments to women and men for the men. For the next forty-five minutes, she felt her way around my body, concentrating on certain meridians that were familiar to me as spots that, when pressed, gave subtle messages that something good was happening. At the end, with the help once again of the interpreter, she suggested that I buy some special dong-6-infused sake from a sake shop not far from the massage school and have two or three sake cups a few times a week.

I felt wonderful, light, and very energized and set off to buy the sake before heading back up the mountain to the hotel. The amazing thing was that I was not interested to take the moving escalator and instead walked all the way up the mountain using the steps, just like the elderly Cantonese women I saw each day. It was a very strong affirmation and confirmation that the traditional *shiatsu* practice of this Asian culture had enormous healing and health benefits. I bought some takeaway food for supper of fried vegetables and rice and sampled the sake, which had an extraordinary taste and powerful effect. My ritual of settling my energy with prayers and gratitude to all to prepare for eating became even more meaningful in the experiences of that day.

The following day, I took the ferryboat across to Southern Lantau Island, as I had been told there was a Buddhist temple that was a must-see. So I packed up lunch, towel, and water for the day and caught the early morning ferry over to the island, which was about a forty-five-minute trip. On arrival, everyone went to get a bus to take them to the shops, restaurants, and tourist attractions, but my inner voice guided me to walk in the opposite direction. And I came upon a trail that meandered all around the southeast coastal side of Lantau, and I naturally took off my sandals and happily walked barefoot.

After about an hour, I came to a small waterfall and could see below that it went all the way down to a secluded beach cove—my perfect lunch and swimming spot. It was quite a steep hillside, but there were plenty of rocks at the sides of the waterfall, and once I was down there, I was in heaven. I had a spectacular view of the islands, boats, and China way off in the distance seen through the heat haze of the day. Afterward, I went back up the hill to rejoin the trail in search of a Buddhist temple that a sign, a little ways back, had pointed to.

The temple was quite small, and there were small bowls of rice, some dried-out and some fresh flowers, and other offerings laid out before the entrance. I said one of the chants that I had memorized, "Hi fu mi yo I mu na ya ko to mo chi ro," a prayer to the union of all sentient beings. It was then time to retrace my steps and head back in time to get the ferry back to Hong Kong Island. I met only one other fellow walker the entire day. My kind of day and I was filled with grace and gratitude.

The next stop on the trip was a week in Rome, Italy. And true to many of the stories one hears about Italians, by the time my taxi pulled up to the entrance of my hotel, I had experienced two proposals of marriage, both of which made me smile but that I gracefully declined.

Rome was pulsing with high energy, though vastly different to the urban energy of Hong Kong, no less stimulating. I visited the Coliseum and the Vatican/Sistine Chapel; took the train to the beach one day and another one to Castel Gandolfo, the Pope's summer residence in the hills a short distance to the south; and generally explored the famous streets of this ancient Roman city.

Finding foods that worked for me was fairly easy, though not quite as satisfying as my experience in Hong Kong. However, one thing that clouded the whole Italian stay was that I experienced a sudden feeling of darkness/depression, which actually began almost the minute I arrived there. And I couldn't shake it off or have clarity of its origin. As soon as I left to return to New York via Frankfurt for a plane change, it disappeared. Two and a half years later, I had a psychic reading done at the College for Intuition in San Rafael, San Francisco, during which a young psychic, who knew nothing of my trip to Rome, told me she saw very clearly that I had been tortured and persecuted in Europe as a witch in 1600/1700.

I arrived back at the Happy Little Trailer after almost three weeks of travel since my departure on September 13, 2001, feeling somewhat exhausted and suffering from a mild case of vertigo but elated. After a few days of adjusting, I had a clear vision of where I wanted to live and immediately began planning to move to Maui, Hawaii.

It seemed that the universe was supporting this plan as with the help of a new man in my life, Evan. I went online to the Maui News classifieds and immediately found a two-bedroom upstairs apartment in the exact location where I wished to live. After a conversation with the owner, it was settled and I would arrive back on Maui to start my new life on November 5.

Chapter 35

Great Changes 2002: New Life, Work, and Relationship in Hawaii

My life in Hawaii began to unfold in all the ways that I had hoped it would. I began a cooking and consulting practice that took off immediately, and many of my clients became new dear friends. I volunteered with a community program and was elected to play a part in the mayor of Maui's Recycling Task Force, which was very interesting and fulfilling to be able to work on a project that is such an important part of who I am and my lifework. Evan came out mid-January, and we took a magical, five-day trip to the big island with my dear, newfound Maui friend, Rene, who was also our island guide.

A seven-week trip to travel back to New York was planned departing early June and included Evan's parents' fiftieth anniversary party, his brother's wedding, and an SHI macrobiotic workshop with Denny Waxman.

Evan left Maui one week ahead of me, and I then learned that I was with child. It was one of the happiest days of my life. I was walking on air for the next four days and then my moon cycle started. I flew to New York to meet up with Evan and it just so happened that Denny Waxman was in New York City, giving consultations, and I was able to get an appointment the following day. He gave several recommendations and was very reassuring, and I left feeling confident that all would be okay somehow. As usual, it was easy and pleasurable to follow Denny's suggestions, which included the special black soybean stew recipe, which has always been a favorite.

Evan and I had already been signed up to attend a three-day strengthening health course with Denny, and ten days later, we set off for Temenos Retreat Center, just west of Philadelphia, Pennsylvania. It was such a wonderful and joyful experience altogether—including and especially that I was able to share it with Evan and that for three full days, I was able to let go of cooking and be fed all the foods (expertly prepared by Denny's eldest son, Joe, and his kitchen staff) that my mind, body, and spirit had come to enjoy and depend on for my best, optimum health and energy.

I especially loved the sauerkraut they served. Well, it took about twelve hours after we got back to the cabin before the penny dropped, and lo and behold, I discovered once again that I was pregnant. The timing was interesting, as that morning, my dear friend Tom Marshall came by with a friend to take away the Happy Little Trailer. His friend's house had burned down and so I had donated the trailer to him to serve as a temporary home. The cabin became my official residence, albeit with quite a few things still to be completed.

The following weeks went by in a blissful haze. A poem came to mind about the new life within me that Evan and I had agreed would be called Jules, whether a girl or boy. I naturally called Denny to share the good news, and he suggested that I avoid watching any strong energy/violent or strange films and also strongly advised against any air travel until after the baby was born. Evan and I were both quite okay about not returning to Maui to insure the baby's safe term and delivery.

I met with the local midwife, whose children Rose had schooled with over the years and all seemed to be well in the progression.

Alas, though, it was a short-lived pregnancy, as seven weeks later—after a happy Saturday spent in Great Barrington, Massachusetts—I awoke in the morning to a voice, saying, "You are no longer with child." And then I started cramping and began to bleed slightly.

I called Denny, and he gave some suggestions, but in the middle of Monday night, the child spirit voice instructed me to go and squat outside on the earth. And I miscarried our baby. It was alternately then one of the saddest days of my life.

The bigger the front, the bigger the back was echoing in my head, as it was one of the most intense emotional and spiritual roller coaster, high-low rides I had ever experienced.

We buried the hardly formed fetus outside the cabin exactly where I had squatted, and Jules is always with me, especially remembered on August 12 of each year, when, with lighted candles, food and prayers are offered to his/her spirit in the traditional Buddhist way.

It was a long, drawn-out miscarriage with a lot of post-contractions, as my body made an effort to completely clean out my womb. And I stayed home at the cabin for almost all the next three weeks, resting and grieving the loss.

Then it was time to restart the projects needed to complete the interior of the cabin. Tom S dropped off his floor stapler so that the previously donated Wisconsin Church tongue-in-groove flooring could be installed. I managed to do the kitchen area but found myself getting deeply fatigued and ended up hiring a lovely, energetic, young couple to finish the rest. They also helped to upgrade the solar system, install a solar-powered motor onto the simple pump well pump, and build an eight-by-twelve-foot studio that later on became the storage and tool shed.

Rose came up one weekend with a few of her friends, and one night, nature gave us a special treat. I was still eating supper, while the others had all gone outside to light a fire and watch the sun setting. Suddenly, they all started making sounds of excitement and wonder, and Evan came rushing in to urge me to go and join them all in witnessing the aurora borealis. Wow! It truly was a spectacular dinner and show and right there on my doorstep.

Chapter 36

Losing Mum

November 21, 2002, just as I was getting back into the flow and feeling optimistic again and after going out to post flyers for a series of cooking classes I was offering, I arrived back at Evan's cottage. (We had given Rose and her boyfriend the cabin for a few weeks.) Evan came out to greet me and asked to carry the shopping in, which in itself was a little strange, but I thought he was trying to make up for an upset that had happened between us earlier in the day. I said that I needed some fresh air, went for a stroll around the small lake to unwind, and then went inside. Evan offered me some freshly made kukicha tea, which I accepted gratefully. And I sat down at the table, while he was seated on the futon sofa. After a few minutes, he then just said simply, "Christina, life has its ups and downs. I am so sorry to tell you that your mother died today."

It was one of the most shocking moments in my life.

I knew that Mummy had tripped up and fallen a few weeks earlier while walking the dog and had gashed her forehead. Then she had been feeling unwell with what was eventually diagnosed as the flu, and my older sister was staying there and helping mum get back on her feet. I had spoken with her the evening before, and she had said Mum was feeling better. She also told me that Mum had had no alcohol for about ten days, and they were having some good conversations due to this, but she also told me that her legs were very swollen, to which I suggested to make a special remedy drink of daikon and carrot and to give her plenty of daikon/turnips or radishes at meals, which she had always enjoyed while I was staying with her.

My sister called the doctor in the next morning, and he had suggested offering her a drink as "after all, she was elderly and she should have a little of what she fancied." Well, that November afternoon, while watching her favorite TV program, *Jeopardy*, Mummy got up to go to the bathroom and collapsed on the floor.

My sister did CPR and called emergency services but to no avail. My mother had suffered a massive heart attack and was pronounced dead on arrival at the hospital. The autopsy report showed that there was no liver disease in my mother, which considering the amount of alcohol she had consumed over the years was very interesting to me. After all, she had apparently been making balance with all the high-fat animal foods that had been her daily fare since birth. It was the high cholesterol and clogged arteries that ended her life at the age of seventy-three.

When my mother died, I found myself literally holding my breath. It wasn't until several weeks later that I realized what I was doing and from then on had to constantly keep reminding myself to purposefully inhale and exhale, and I still have to up to this day. Since healing myself, for the most part, cooking and eating food had become my way of celebrating life, but from the moment I heard of Mum's death, I lost my appetite and only wanted to eat unusually small portions of very simple food, which kept leaving me feeling hungry, cold, and sad. I simply didn't feel like celebrating her departure. I decided to ask Denny Waxman for his advice, and he gave some helpful suggestions, including that I go to a warmer climate again to help relax. He suggested also that I buy some very special sake and drink two, three, or four little cups, however much it took for me to take a deep breath and release an *ah* of satisfaction. I added the forty-nine-day Buddhist prayer ritual for departed loved ones, which includes the lighting of two white candles and fresh offerings of water, rice, and salt.

It took me a good two years to go through the grieving period and during that time, through conscious practice, discovered the true *ah* of both breathing and eating—in other words, taking both to the place of always feeling deeply satisfied. It wasn't until just a few months ago—during a session with my male therapist—that a light bulb went off about the big reaction I had to my mother dying. It became clear that I had not ever properly grieved for the loss and abandonment I surely must have experienced in early childhood when Dad left and Mummy was recovering from her breakdown/loss/abandonment.

My grandmother, mimicking what her governesses said to her, would often say to us children, "Cry and you cry alone. Laugh and the whole world laughs with you." And so I learned from a young age to bottle up the tears (along with most other emotions also). I realized that when Mum died, my spirit insisted that I take as much time as I needed to really feel my feelings and go through the process of loss without distraction or denial. I am grateful over and over again for the gift of listening and hearing my inner voice.

Chapter 37

Life after Mum and the Book

Soon afterward, that voice said very loudly and clearly, "Write your book." It's been an ongoing niggling reminder, but it propelled me slowly but surely forward.

Another voice message said that I needed to find a tantric teacher. And within two weeks of arriving back on Maui, in January 2003, Joan and Tomas Heartfield came into my life, and I started studying with them, taking part in a ten-week program. I was blown away by what I learned and the things that I experienced emotionally/mentally, spiritually, and physically. I feel such great gratitude to them both for sharing their wisdom, great compassion, care, and empathy. And I always keep connected with them telepathically and join in a day workshop whenever I can when I am on Maui during the winter months. The study of tantric and Taoist healing and energy leave no doubt in my mind that this has played and keeps playing an essential part in working through past and present trauma. It seems to be a key component in relationship to and with knowing and loving myself. It helps me in all areas of relationships with others.

It was very hard to relax and allow after Mum died. I became ultrasensitive. It was a spiritual shock, and I became thin-skinned and weakened. I began to realize what an enormous influence she had on me. She had been so amazingly supportive when I was ill, both emotionally and physically, by carrying heavy bags of shopping for me back up the steep hill from the town. She sent out constant prayers to me and my siblings and had unconditional love. She was not obsessive despite her difficulties. She had a hard time under my grandmother's influence/control, and she'd been on her own as a single woman/parent for forty-one years, ever since Dad left us all in January 1962. I have only had a few dreams of being with her over these past eighteen years since she left this earthly world, and all of them are very real encounters.

I have also noticed that there are some interesting life-changing experiences that I seem to have duplicated / have in common with my mother:

We both had a bit of a rocky start.

We were both given raw, unpasteurized, full-cream cow's milk with sugar at birth.

We both had bad/decaying teeth from a young age.

At the age of thirty-two years, we both suffered a great shock/change/illness.

We had subsequent shocking experiences that made our hair fall out several years later.

We often both seemed to get on the wrong side of MM. (Though happily, my relationship with MM changed dramatically!)

Mum always swept/mopped the kitchen floor in the morning before breakfast as do I.

Mum and I both enjoyed/enjoy spending time with and caring for elders.

In addition, MM was advised by her doctor to have a little whiskey with orange juice in the evening in order to help her relax. It had sounded familiar when Denny suggested I do the same.

It seemed clear that I needed to be in a warmer climate for the winter months, but it also felt right to go back home to my cabin property for the warmer months. So I started to make an effort to divide my life into two parts: summer/autumn in Upstate New York cabin life and winter/spring in warmer climate life.

To help afford and justify being away in the winter months, I started to rent out the cabin to different folks. Musicians, artists, writers, and carpenters have, for the most part, all graced my property during my absences. Once the cabin was more or less completed and I had the water and solar systems installed, I started to invite close family and friends to stay as a way for them to step back from the world and be in a beautiful unspoilt mountainous retreat setting.

Chapter 38

Lyme Disease

In the summer of 2005 whilst at the cabin, a huge, purple rash appeared on my ass and I had flu symptoms along with a fever of 104 degrees Fahrenheit for several days. It was initially diagnosed as a spider bite.

I used all my macrobiotic remedies and finally got the fever to break only to wake up to the feeling that a metal stake was being pushed through the right side of my head. Once again, I felt as if I was surely dying. Evan went back online and discovered that all my symptoms indicated that I had Lyme disease and should probably get onto antibiotics ASAP. I called Denny Waxman, who highly recommended that I do so, as he had seen many people having great difficulties by trying to treat the disease by avoiding using antibiotics. He reminded me of my highly sensitive nature.

I immediately followed his advice and within twelve hours, was feeling so much better. Furthermore, whatever had been upsetting my digestive system over the past year was cured. Unfortunately, I have now been infected with Lyme disease multiple times, with each recurring bout manifesting in different, initially puzzling, symptoms: a really stiff neck that travels and then debilitates, a painful elbow or shoulder that also then travels either into the wrist/hand or across the upper back, flu-like symptoms, and one occasion, a strange rash that traveled from one side of my face across to the other. Each time I go through another episode, I think I have a handle on diagnosing. And each time, I am at first bewildered until I realize it's Lyme again doing its impersonating act.

I take a kudzu-root (with or without umeboshi) drink weekly and sometimes a round of Chinese herbal tea and take antibiotics when needed. Because Lyme is very prevalent in Upstate New York and that is my real home, I realized that I needed to equip myself and adapt to cope with this disease in order to keep enjoying my mountain cabin life. I make an essential oil blend of lavender and rose-geranium-and-lemon balm and spray my body and clothing before going outside, reapplying often. For the most part, it has been doing the trick quite well in keeping the ticks away.

On August 23, 2005, Hurricane Katrina hit the Gulf Coast and New Orleans was devastated. I found an organization online that had set up in the worst affected area and made a mental note to find out how I might be able to volunteer to be of use in some way, somehow, once I had clarity of my winter movement—maybe offering my cooking services.

Once I was back on my feet after the Lyme incident, after doing a little research, I bought a 2001 Ford Econoline Falcon camper van. It had been on my wish list for many years to be able to live the gypsy life and travel around with my home on my back, so to speak. The added initiative was that Rose, then newly engaged, wanted me to go out to Los Angeles that Christmas to meet the parents of her fiancé with whom she was staying.

Evan joined me, and we set off for California in early December and had an interesting maiden voyage. After the family gathering, we spent the next three months exploring the West Coast area, and on the return journey in March, we got some dental work done just over the border into Mexico near Yuma, Arizona. Evan flew up to Northern California to help a mutual friend in need, and I continued heading East, solo. I had contacted the hurricane relief group in New Orleans and went to volunteer some time with them in the Ninth Ward. I found traveling in the van made my personal practice and pace ever more useful. I would keep up with my morning rituals, making sure that I prepared any food that would be needed for the day and after taking a half-hour walk, set off for driving a maximum of five hours a day.

Chapter 39

New Orleans

The time that I spent in New Orleans in the wake of Hurricane Katrina was an eye-opener to say the least. The group that I volunteered with had manifested the most spectacular support. There were two huge circus-size tents: One was the dining meals room, and the other was the kitchen. Several dozen refrigerated two- and three-axle trailer trucks were running their generators twenty-four seven. There were dozens of solar panels powering some of the electrical equipment, multiple generators, and smaller tents for all the donations that were still pouring in from all over the country and indeed, the world—tents for clothing (separate one for men, women, and children), household items, medical needs, books, pet care, personal, hair, and beauty products.

I was blown away by how organized they all were, and when I checked in was asked what my skills were, I offered to make a couple of large loaves of my special, whole-wheat sourdough bread, which was greeted with warm enthusiasm. The majority of the foods that were donated were prepackaged commercial brands, and anything homemade on the spot was considered very special. That night, I set the bread to sour and rise and baked the two loaves, Dutch-oven style on the two burners in the camper. I slept to the hum of the generators. I also carried two extra portable butane cooking stoves that enabled other dishes to be cooked that were needed for the day.

In the afternoons, I also volunteered to give some counseling in one of the therapeutic tents and spent some time listening to the stories of several people who had wandered in for the day for food and support.

The area was like a ghost town, but just as nature does its thing in the seasons, new shoots were sprouting up all over the place. When I took my morning walk in the fields near the organization's location, which were still mostly completely covered in silt from the flooding seven months earlier, I was heartened to see that there were new, strong, green shoots determined to reach the sunlight.

The majority of the homes and buildings were ruined, but there were signs of repair and rebuilding here and there. Most of the electricity in this district was still out—no traffic lights, no night lights—so all driving was done using an unspoken care and consideration code. Anyone who arrived at the intersection first was offered/given preference to move ahead. One or two businesses were trying to reopen to help restart commerce in the community, and it just so happened that the camper was in great need of an oil change and one tire seemed to have a slow leak. So on the morning of my departure, I became customer number one at John's Auto that had just reopened for business that day. A mere twenty minutes away, I was stepping into a whole foods market in an area that had been hardly affected by the storm—the proximity of the contrast was astounding.

The whole experience of my time spent there was very humbling and rewarding, and I felt honored to have had the privilege of stepping into join in such a magnificent act of community care and outpouring of love.

Chapter 40

Seasonal Commutes and Ongoing Cabin Projects

The following years were spent in between the cabin in the spring and summers and during the winters, traveling around in the camper in the Southern warmer states—often parking at my brother's country property in Sarasota, Florida, and sometimes leaving the camper there or with friends in Phoenix, Arizona, and flying over to Maui, Hawaii, for a few weeks. Evan went to live and help out with his aging parents in Queens, New York, and we got together here or there.

Several local handypersons, the father and sons of some dear neighbors, and a variety of builders came to help in a variety of projects. My brother had strongly suggested that I put a metal roof on the cabin and any other structures as a practical and safety measure, and that was completed. A woodshed was made out of wood builders' palettes, a metal roof and the front covered with a hanging Army cotton oiled tarpaulin. I had made a feng shui mistake for the main cabin entrance, decided to take out two of the mountain northwest-facing windows and screens, and installed a lovely set of French doors, with the expert help and guidance from Tom S. We dismantled the old tent platform that George and his friends had made in the early years and used most of it to create the floor for a beautiful, tiny eight-foot-by-eight-foot guest cottage with a hip roof. And the windows and screens taken out of the cabin were put in to create one whole wall of light! We gathered plenty of large flat stones to help create a beautiful stone floor for the outside shower. Two new oak trees were planted to replace the two that were cut down that were leaning precariously close to the cabin. The pond area needed to be rechinked as the rainwater was seeping back into the ground too quickly and there were plenty of newts and frogs that would go somewhere else for lack of it. And their presence adds great pleasure!

"One regret dear world, that I am determined not to have when I am lying on my deathbed is that I did not kiss you enough."

—Hefiz of Persia

The official opening ceremony of the cabin: Summer 2010

After the installation of the metal roof and the new double French doors on the cabin, I felt it was time to have a potluck party to thank all the folks who helped build the cabin and outbuildings and gave support in any way over the years. Charlie brought over his oven on wheels so that we could bake bread outdoors on the rock. People played music, ate, and reminisced, and the cabin was officially named the Taj Mahal.

I really couldn't thank enough all who played a part in providing me my home—including especially Paul and Jodi; Charlie and his son, Rob; Tom M; Lou at the recycling center; Tom S; Manna Jo; Sam; Tim; Andi; Timothy; George; Irene; the Birch family; and all my other great neighbors. It was a lovely gathering, and I was filled with love and gratitude for these wonderful, generous broad/macro-minded friends.

Chapter 41

Life Changes

In January 2008, my monthly cycles began to fade out. It was a sad time in my life, and I am possibly one of only a few people who grieves this extraordinary potentially procreational natural event. There were no uncomfortable hot flashes. Instead, I became extra emotional, and it seemed that my hormones were in outrage at the upset. I still miss my quiet moon days spent peacefully feeling the wonder of my body's fullness, but I am so very grateful that I was, after all, able to truly experience its occurrence after the eight-year absence during my illness and eventual recovery.

Sometime during this changing time in my life, I attended a classical guitar recital at the opening of a new bookshop in Kingston, New York. A book called *Journey of the Heart* by John Welwood almost fell onto my lap while I was leaning on the bookshelf next to my seat. I scanned the first few paragraphs and knew that I needed to buy it.

The following day, as I began reading, a bright and wonderful light turned on in my mind as I was introduced to the concept of validation as a key component of communication and peace in the world. Through the simple act of validation of self and of others in each and all our own experiences, we could generate greater compassion and empathy for all. I realized that all I had to do from then on was to begin to separate myself from anybody else's experience and take responsibility for my reaction and experience in relation to them and theirs.

It has been a work in progress ever since as I continue to practice validation with each and every person I encounter and witness their reaction to be really listened to and heard. I went on to read another book by John Welwood, *Love and Awakening,* and learned that the greatest challenge with this practice is with closest family members, relatives, and friends who will (no doubt) trigger me/us to many past experiences—mostly from a young age, when we were not validated and consequently had a reaction that served to help us get through that time. Once we are able to have this realization, the healing begins. My empathy and compassion of all grows daily, and I am once again humbled in my places of ignorance / not knowing and grateful for these/my life lessons.

Chapter 42

Hurricane Sandy: October 28, 2012

I was at the cabin on my own when Hurricane Sandy barreled up the Northeast coast and naturally got ready for the predicted very strong winds and mayhem that it might cause. Having weathered quite a few storms up there in the mountains, I did not feel too concerned but knew that this was going to be on a much bigger scale and went about making preparations. I parked the camper in the center of the cul-de-sac at the entrance to the driveway, out of the way of any overhanging tree branches. I secured all the cabin windows that were closed from the outside with large number-sixteen nails, keeping in mind that all the windows and doors were old-fashioned, single-pane storm windows and only the new, double-opening French doors were double glazed. I was going to pray hard they would withstand the onslaught of seventy-miles-per-hour-plus winds. I also wrapped a rope around the woodshed and tarp door to stop it flapping and ripping and put anything that was vulnerable inside the storage studio.

At first, it started off tame enough and then it hit the area full force. And I just sat inside the cabin in awe of the majesty and power of nature, watching forty-foot pine trees bending in what seemed to be a most unnatural degree. The winds howled around the cabin for hours, then it all went quiet, and I knew I was sitting right in the middle of the eye of the storm until it all started up again and even stronger than before. Wow, it was amazing to witness.

What was even more amazing was that the only damage that the cabin suffered was from rainwater that was forced by the wind up and under the northeastern bedroom window and which soaked the burlap wall covering underneath it on the inside. There is still a watermark there today, which I call the Sandy mark. There was only one largish tree branch that had come down along the lane, and that was it. A miracle because when I went out driving two days later, I discovered that hundreds of huge trees had been toppled and on my walk deep in the woods a few days after, found a whole line of about fifteen trees had all gone down when one of the several tornadoes that came through as part of the storm had pushed them over like a row of skittles

Because the area is very rocky, the trees often have shallow roots, and these toppled ones created giant root walls. They are still there today, though somewhat disintegrated back into the earth. I felt very lucky and was extremely grateful that not one single glass pane or roof was damaged.

Chapter 43

February 2014: Sharing Macrobiotics with My Daughter in a Whole New Way

My daughter, Rose, had been suffering from chronic and severe migraine headaches for seven years. She had already seen Denny Waxman during her first trimester of her pregnancy back in 2007, and during that time, I was able to stay with her and her husband and prepare many of the dishes that he recommended for her. The migraines abated for the rest of her pregnancy but returned when her son was about six months old.

During the next five years, she visited many health practitioners from both allopathic and alternative modes and sometimes had some initial improvement but nothing that was so significantly remarkable that she eventually succumbed to some strong prescription pills. She had gotten herself into a tight corner with all sorts of dietary restrictions, and she was not happy with her health. I had noticed for some years that her skin color had a gray, unhealthy tone and prayed that she would eventually be guided to the right person who would help her understand her condition. In July of the previous year, Rose and her family had moved from New Jersey to California.

I felt optimistic that the move would help bring about some relaxed changes in Rose's health and had one small sign when I first stayed with them in their beach cottage at the end of August 2013. I had been incorporating the sweet vegetable drink that Denny had recommended I take for a few months and offered some to Rose on the second morning when she was having a particularly bad migraine. The result was great.

She said that something had just relaxed in the area under her heart for the first time in years. I told her that was her spleen/pancreas area and so began a small new opening. I shared the drink with her for the rest of my stay and showed her how to make it, suggesting that she take it once to twice daily for a couple of weeks and then taper off to less often, having fresh carrot juice mix on in between days. She found it helpful for her blood sugar dips and sweet cravings, but the headaches persisted.

A week before I was due to arrive in California in February the following year, Denny had contacted me about submitting my story for his new website. It turned out that he was going to be in the Santa Monica area the same week as I was and would be available for consultations for one day. I called Rose and offered her a revisit consult with Denny, if she felt he might once again help her deal with her migraines, and she accepted. On the Thursday, Rose, her husband, and I went to see him.

His recommendations were simple and clear: Animal food was the main cause, and a need for a regulated daily lifestyle would be most helpful. Rose felt that what he said was accurate. I was relieved by his recommendations and felt very optimistic.

I offered to extend my stay by an extra two weeks in order that I might better help her get going with the special remedy drinks and the daily food suggestions, and this was accepted. And miraculously, the airline did not charge a penalty.

During those two weeks, I shared myself wholeheartedly in the best way I knew to through the most accurate interpretation and preparation of Denny's recommended dietary suggestions as I could do. Rose started doing the daily body rub and drank and ate all that I prepared, and on the second day, she came into the kitchen with a smile on her face and said, "Mummy, I feel so much better." And I noticed also that her gray skin color had changed to a more naturally healthy tone. On the third day, the same thing happened, and Rose said how well she felt. And then her husband came in and said, "I was skeptical, but it's obviously working because Rose looks so much healthier and is so much happier already."

As the days progressed, once my grandboy had been taken to school, Rose joined me in the kitchen in the mornings for cooking classes with mother and using her iPhone, videoed and photographed the various stages of the dishes she was learning how to prepare. I should add that she has usually preferred not to have to cook for herself but was always a willing co-cook with me at her side. This new level of her actually wanting to understand how to make delicious food that would make her healthier and happy made me incredibly grateful. At last, I was being able to pass on the health-giving gift of macrobiotics to my own daughter.

I had been aware for so long that she had been born through my pathological condition, and even though I had had the opportunity to heal my own birth condition, I had not, up to this point, been able to inspire her to seek the same. She made a commitment to follow the macrobiotic way for one year. The miracle of this story is that she had been two months migraine-pill free and fully committed to the task of preparing food for herself and her family to the best of her ability. I loved getting the photos she shared with me of various dishes she had just cooked, and it was clear that she is indeed a very good cook. She became more relaxed and happy and even though she has not, so far, remained completely migraine free, has to date been able to manage her condition better.

Chapter 44

My Sewing Hat

My love of fine fabrics and creating practical and beautiful garments has filled my life with an extra sweet and creative dimension since the age of seven when I first learned how to thread a needle and sew embroidery stitches onto a yellow gingham apron. More recently, over the past few years, I have taken on several special dressmaking and sewing projects. Three wedding dresses for my daughter, younger sister, and niece have kept me very focused and honed my skills as a seamstress in a wonderful way. I was flown out to Edinburgh for my sister's wedding that was held in a Scottish castle and beautiful grounds, and I naturally traveled with my own food, which was easily supplemented with delicious Scottish salmon, wedding cake, fresh Atlantic halibut, and local vegetables. Then two years ago, I found myself staying in Hackney, London, for my niece's wedding and again had plenty of prepared basic foods that kept me in balance during all the excitement of the occasion!

I am always still so amazed and grateful that I have both the ability to create fine clothing and then especially be able to join in with the big social family gatherings, even though I need lots of recovery and quiet time at the other end of it all.

These days, I am fashioning facial masks in an effort to comply with the guidelines for social safety and distancing during the COVID-19 pandemic

Chapter 45

Around the World Again! Western United States of America Trip: Eastern Around the World Trip

In September 2019, I bought my second upgraded camper van as a joint venture with dear friends in New York in order to be able to comfortably visit with friends and family in Colorado, New Mexico, and California. Three months and seven thousand miles later, I dropped the van off with my friends in time to set off in an easterly direction to go back (actually forward) to Maui for the winter and where I was planning to work diligently to finish writing this book. Toting the Coleman rolling cooler bag packed tightly with my specially prepared foods to last the four-day journey, I traveled around the planet from JFK to Kiev to Delhi to Oahu and finally onto Maui. It was once again a great experience.

I have continued working on the ongoing projects while at the cabin and the solar system was upgraded to run twenty-four volts and extra batteries added to the battery bank. A second larger system was installed this year, which will feed the tiny new guest studio and allow the super new three-way fridge to run on solar during long sunny daytime hours, thereby saving on propane usage.

Practices

As the earth's energy moves in an ever-changing quickening direction, I have learned that in order to keep apace, it seems more vitally important to be diligent in my personal practices, especially yoga and taking the daily walk, which is so very balancing and helps me to clear my mind and listen to my inner voice for lifestyle and dietary updates. For example, compared to thirty years ago, these days, I eat less grains, more light grains, more oil, include more relaxing side dishes, drinks, and sweeter type of sake.

I get shiatsu, bodywork, and acupuncture treatments as needed and have found them all to be most beneficial, especially if I have Lyme disease recurring symptoms.

I periodically get blood work, mammogram, and pap smears done so that I can have diagnosis from an allopathic point of view just to make sure that all is in balance.

Chapter 46

Cook, Pray, Eat

Taking time to eat and the advanced art of chewing

Excerpt from *The Lost Diary of Don Juan* by Douglas Carlton Abrams (Washington Square Press):

> I am always amazed at our willingness to eat casually in public, given how secretive we are about our other bodily appetites. The act of ingestion is as intimate and, when truly enjoyed, as sensual. (Douglas Carlton Abrams, *The Lost Diary of Don Juan*, page 135–6)

Mealtimes represent who I wish/need to be in this lifetime: grateful, calm, serene, peaceful, fun, energetic, and contented. And I know I already said it, but need to say it again, *grateful.*

If I am unable to give myself the ingredients that support me in this way, both in food and environment, my spirit is unsettled and not happy.

I strive to make sure that I always give myself plenty of time to have unhurried meals taken on time. The earlier the better. And I have found that I need to spend a certain (the same) amount of time each day eating and chewing carefully in order to achieve the ideal nutrient quota and to sustain my inner calm and clear mindedness. I make my life work for me around my schedule rather than allowing the world's schedule to dictate mine—i.e., most appointments are made for the afternoon hours so that I have had plenty of time to do the food preparation for the day, take my walk, and eat lunch peacefully. Funnily enough, I find I can nearly always eat my meals on time when traveling.

The ah/aum/ohm of eating and chewing: Cook, pray, eat

There is no doubt in my mind that eating is a sacred act—that all food is sacred as is the life it nourishes.

Mealtimes are a very special time for me, and once I sit down to eat, I neither like nor wish to get up or be interrupted in any way as this upsets my energy flow in this important process.

All food is nectar to me, and consciously eating and chewing is a deeply sensual experience. Something very magical happens in my mind, body, and spirit with every mouthful.

Everything I eat is chewed until it is liquid, and all liquids I drink are also chewed. Occasionally, I will count to see how many times I am, in fact, chewing these days; and it is generally between forty and sixty times. That is to say they are swilled/mixed with saliva and tasted well before swallowing.

My eyes always close automatically during the prayers before I eat and for much of the time, while I am eating, usually just opening to get a new mouthful. Any other time they want to open, they just do naturally. I presume this is a built-in reflex that certainly helps me to relax and more fully enjoy the sensuality of the process.

The exception to my eyes opening is if I am disturbed during a mealtime.

At first, a wonderful, warm, soothing sensation floods my head/brain area. As I continue to break down the food, the sensation moves down my throat and neck area. And as I begin to finally start swallowing the, by now, liquid nourishment, the sensation descends further into my chest and continues down into my stomach/hara. It always happens and makes me feel so happy and grateful and feels like a divine act. The longer I chew, the more delicious the food

163

becomes and the greater the sensation. And sometimes it's hard to actually swallow a mouthful that keeps flooding my senses with pleasure. I call it the *aum/ohm* of eating, and often, I will feel so delighted by the flavor/taste/sensation of a food I am eating that I chant sounds of enjoyment. And at the end of meals, I will often let out an *ah* of satisfaction and say thank-you in gratitude.

This sweet message and connection with food helps me encourage people to take time to be quiet and switch everything off to be able to chew and listen. Something will speak to you if you keep practicing this art of eating. The key is slowing down.

We have thirty-two teeth, and each one is connected to the thirty-two vertebrae and our digestive, respiratory, and nervous system. As soon as we put food in our mouth, the slightly salty saliva miraculously is secreted to help in the breaking down of the food, which serves to alkalinize everything in preparation for going into the stomach. When preparing vegetables and fruits by cutting/slicing/grating and pickling/salting them, we are activating the beneficial enzymes. The process of chewing further activates this vital process. This simple natural act of chewing sends vibrations through the whole circulatory system, gently massaging the whole spinal cord. (Amazing huh?)

It seems clear to me that in order to properly massage our system, we need to chew for certain amount of time each mouthful/meal/each day. So it's maybe easier to see another subtler reason why some people want to keep eating more and more for comfort because they don't know how important it is to chew. They simply are trying to get the massaging-the-nervous-system effect by putting more food in.

I often will get strong insights and clear messages as I am quietly chewing both solid food and liquids. I seem to gain greater insight on a variety of topics.

One of these powerful messages repeats with some regularity, especially when I hear of various states of war, disease, and general pathology in the world news. The message is simply that if the whole world knew what I have been blessed to learn/know, I believe there would likely be peace, harmony, and great health on this, our earthly, magical planet and we would all be in a sacred state of bliss. We would all be constantly downloading truth and information for living just lives.

If you haven't already totally gotten into chewing everything until it's liquid, you might try to take some quiet time to yourself to practice chewing (a snack of a few nuts or a carrot stick are good examples). You may start to really feel more satisfied on less food as you begin to (a) assimilate and digest better and (b) start massaging your central nervous, digestive, and circulatory systems.

I have recently calculated, in a moment of curiosity, that since 1986, when I first started purposefully/consciously eating, I have spent approximately thirty-five thousand hours in prayerful chewing. That is taking into account the approximately two and a half hours by three meals a day. It works out to be one thousand hours per year.

Breathing and prayers / grace before eating

Prayers before eating started out as a way to settle my energy after cooking and found I could not take a bite of food until I was really calm and settled. Feeling so grateful for having discovered this magical act of chewing and the effect it produced in body mind and spirit, I wanted to say thank-you to all. After a while, once I had stabilized my condition and was no longer in a place of feeling starved for many so years, I then seemed to spend less time on this ritual and said the prayers quite quickly without paying too much attention to what I was saying, but it always settled me enough to then begin eating. In the spring of 2005 after returning to Hawaii, I felt myself going too fast in the world and eating more overstimulating food. And one afternoon, I went into that familiar shocked place where my body suddenly rebelled and my heart started racing, and it felt as though all my energy was stuck in my upper body. I also began to experience what I felt was an intestinal upset where everything seemed to be going through my system too quickly, and some mornings after emptying my bowels, I was so fearful that I would not ever be able to rebuild/replenish my energy. It felt as though I was leaking chi. I struggled to regain balance over the next few days but then my adrenals shut down. I could barely leave the house for days, and in the weeks that followed, I was forced to be quiet and listen and found myself really needing to focus on what I was eating and the adjustments I needed to make in my practice and cooking. That included especially focusing on the prayers before eating as a way to settle and bring my energy down/into my body. Once again, I came to understand my condition better.

So ever since that time, it usually takes me five to ten minutes to settle myself before being/feeling ready to eat. I make sure that there are no sounds that will bother me, and if in a room with a noisy fridge, I will turn it off. And I always switch off the phone ringer. I then take big, deep breaths, feeling the oxygen relax my mind and body. I usually drink a little kukicha tea and sometimes beer or sake in the evening and then begin the prayers:

I give thanks for this food that I have been blessed with, and I truly hope that I am worthy of it. I hope that I have earned and am deserving of it.

I pray for all those who are less fortunate—who may have little or nothing to eat—that they might be supported and nourished in the best possible ways.

I give thanks to all those involved in the growing, harvesting, production, and distribution (shipping, trucking, selling) of this food and for giving me the ability to buy, cook, share, and eat it and to those for cooking and serving of it if I am eating out.

I give thanks to all my ancestors on both my mother and father's side, for all they have gone through before me throughout the ages.

I pray for all sentient beings—all creatures great and small, all living things affected by natural and unnatural conditions—that they might be honored and supported in the best possible ways.

I give thanks for my family, friends, and the whole world. I pray we can all grow together in peace, love, good health, harmony, and understanding with consideration, gratitude, and forgiveness— humbly, joyfully, authentically, integrally, appropriately, respectfully, responsibly. Compassionately with hearts open, caring, and generous. And consciously with minds expanded, aware, evolving. And empathically, relating to and validating ourselves and each other in all our own and each other's experiences.

I pray for justice, equality, and freedom for all that the world/ we become more and more essentially macrobiotic beginning here with me.

Each prayer is repeated twice, sometimes more, until I really feel the prayers and empty my mind of all other thoughts that tend to distract. Once I have settled my energy, letting go of all the business of my day and general concerns, and with empty mind, only then can I comfortably take the first mouthful. On a rare occasion, I will take a spoonful of soup or mouthful of grain, but it rarely feels right to continue eating until I have fully relaxed and connected with the sacred act of eating. I nearly always have to gently ease my way into eating, starting with the mildest-tasting, longer-cooked soft foods, and once those have satisfied that level of hunger, I can then become bolder and eat lighter and crunchier ones. The only time I just say a quick thank-you before eating is when I have an occasional snack or dessert. I generally end the meal with a deep breath of satisfaction and say thank-you once again to the universe.

I discovered years ago when I first started healing a simple formula, which when followed, helped me to let go of overeating foods that were somewhat addictive. And by eating grain throughout the entire meal as the pivot, or foundation, I will feel completely satisfied by the balancing nature of the different food categories. I do not like to mix the different dishes and usually serve them all in individual bowls. I also do not like textures to be mixed, preferring crunchy ones to be separate from soft ones. They have such different and mixed messages/energy. I have found, personally, that soup is best taken at either lunch or supper (though very occasionally, my body asks for it at breakfast), so I generally like to drink the broth first as it serves to further relax me and then eat any vegetables/grain/beans after. Next, I take a mouthful of grain (though again, occasionally, my body asks for a mouthful of veggies/beans dish first to also relax further) followed by the longest-cooked vegetable / bean-vegetable dish, then back to a mouthful of grain. And this gets repeated, going through the different side dishes from longest cooked to shortest. The last mouthful still continues to dance with me.

Salad or lightly steamed greens keeps me peppy and grain grounds me, and I fluctuate between the two as they complement each other and sometimes compete to have the final say. Even when, on occasion, I think I don't want greens, preferring to eat more of the softer comfort foods, I find myself still hungry until I have had at least a couple of mouthfuls of salad or steamed greens. Then everything shifts, and I feel properly satisfied. It's such a pleasure to eat in this way, and I feel nourished and satisfied, ready to carry on with the day's activities without thinking of/about food until the next meal is due to be prepared or warmed up.

My present life

Nowadays, I am, for the most part, automatically guided to what to eat for each activity and purpose, rarely having to stop to try and figure it out. Instead, I have a strong intuition of what I need instead of being guided by my pathological or intellectual condition. I start to get messages to make adjustments and/or changes to my diet that I need to pay attention to, and even though my intuition is working better and better as the years progress, I prefer not to think I am 100 percent right, so with any stubborn stage or condition I usually check in with Denny and seek his advice. He nearly always gives confirmation of things that I have already begun to change/incorporate but generally adds some special ideas that I may or may not have thought of but been unsure if I was on the right track.

As the days and weeks and months and years go by, my practice of taking time to eat and my way of eating continues to help me see things more clearly and serves to allow me even greater freedom to expand and stretch in my life in all ways possible, with more certainty that I am being true to myself and my path no matter how unconventional or strange it may seem to others.

On the subject of dreams/dreaming

When I first started reading about the macrobiotic way, I pondered several ideas. One of those was that dreaming was considered to be a symptom of imbalance or ill health.

Later on, when I was going through my healing time, I read that Tibetan Buddhists, along with others, believe that the spirit rises up out of the body slightly when we are asleep and we then can experience spiritual dreamtime as the spirit travels into another dimensions.

From my personal experience, I think there are at least two types of dream conditions: The first is manifested from a pathological condition, and the second is manifest from a spiritual place.

If I watch a strange sci-fi or aggressive film or eat refined sugar or dairy, I might well have a nightmare or mixed-up, strange dreams that really have no meaning or message. On the other hand, I can have sweet, happy, interesting dreamtimes when I really feel I am experiencing some special events.

I have also had, so far, two premonition dreams of death. Interestingly enough, it involved a related married couple. I was staying with my great-aunt and uncle in the county of Kent, United Kingdom, helping out whilst they were hosting an archaeological dig on their land for students at Oxford University. Aunt M told me of the local superstition that anyone who disturbed the area would die.

Not taking it too seriously, I spent the week helping her to feed and look after the guests. I awoke one morning after a vivid dream that my aunt had died and when I went to her room with her breakfast tray, met my Uncle A who said she had died in the night. Several years later, when we had recently moved to Florida, I had a dream that Uncle A had died. My elder sister called me the next day to give the news that he had in fact died.

When I first started reading about macrobiotics and had not ever met nor seen a photo of Michio Kushi, I had a dream that I met him at the Kushi Institute in Becket, Massachusetts, outside on a big lawn. He told me in the dream that I should really take care fixing my teeth. Well, my teeth were a mess, and I was in a lot of pain when eating. And I hadn't the funds to get anything done. On one occasion, when I visited my family in the United Kingdom, my elder sister urged my grandmother to lend/give me some money to help pay for the dental work needed. And that's what happened. More gratitude.

On the other hand, my dreams are usually very wonderful and often involve meeting up with departed loved ones. I can also experience flying, though I haven't had that dream in a few years now.

It's also very interesting to me that the only time that I dream about food is on the odd occasion when I either haven't eaten enough or I ate too simply or narrowly (i.e., lacking oil/richness/variety) or didn't have a pudding or relaxant. This might happen when I have had a difficult time in settling and relaxing to eat after a big social or distressing event.

"The world is so full of a number of things I am sure we should all be as happy as kings" (Robert Louis Stevenson).

These days, I marvel at the wonders of the world and of all that surrounds me daily. I ponder the power of the planet and all its inhabitants. I am in awe of the abilities of nature and humans to both create and to destroy, only to recreate and on and on—the never-ending cycle of life.

I feel gratitude for each and every person who has played a part in helping my lifework—the food grown, the clothing made, the furniture in my home, the car, the bottles, the roads, the bridges, the buildings, and the airplanes. And it's still such a miracle to dial/punch a few numbers on a telephone and speak to someone thousands of miles away. I think I can more easily understand the energy of an almond than how a telephone can connect people over such a great distances.

"There's always something." My saying.

When I really think about this little saying, it makes me smile! After all, no matter what happens, there is always something.

"There's a little bit of everything in everything."

I have noticed two peculiar similarities within my body.

The first is that an ear looks just like an embryo, and secondly, when I have what I call a perfect poo/bowel movement, it appears to look exactly like a man's penis.

"The bigger the front, the bigger the back." A Taoist saying.

Since I first started to address and heal my birth condition, I began to notice how everything seems indeed to have a front and a back, an opposite on the other side, naturally—night and day, summer and winter, forward and backward, happy and sad, up and down, full and empty.

Looking back to my childhood, it was spent in a highly social structure with an endless stream of visitors and guests at home and surrounded by hundreds of fellow students and teachers during the educational years. From a very young age, I was trying to both soothe my nervous system and also escape from the stress of it all.

On the other side of it, I sought and found, in my Upstate New York property, the total peace, quiet aloneness, and serenity that I needed. So far, I have spent thirty-nine years in socially stressful places and now twenty-five years in a quiet, peaceful place. With luck, I will get to spend at least another fourteen years to complete the natural balance.

Recent dental experience

An interesting thing happened in my health, which I believe was directly connected to a rather traumatic dental ordeal. A front tooth root had cracked, and there was a bad infection that seemed to be traveling up my face. And fearing it might get deeper in my system, I ended up taking clindamycin antibiotics for five days. It turned out that I had an allergic reaction to that particular antibiotic and felt so ill, I thought I might, once again, die.

After confirming this with my dentist, I immediately stopped taking the pills and then called Denny for his advice. At the time, I had felt that every single gram of good bacteria/flora had been wiped out of my gut and intestines, and I was experiencing more pain in my mouth and head than I had ever had in my life and wondered how I would ever rebuild and come out of/through that.

It seems, however, that I had either, once again, been carrying/ hosting some old energy and bacteria and/or Lyme had entered my gut because afterward, my whole digestive system began working in the most optimal way that I had experienced since being on a macrobiotic diet for twenty-six years. Along with Denny's recommendation of kuzu/ume drink and my regular inclusion of miso soup, good-quality pickles, tempeh and sourdough bread, and toasted nori, I also began to include a particular new yoga pose/exercise that my daughter gave me to add into my daily morning yoga, which seemed to trigger some new energy flow. And my condition shifted to a new further place of being more relaxed and open.

The dental issue also forced me to, once again, chew and eat in a different way (to avoid pain). And even doing that, I felt and still feel, more gentle and balanced. I couldn't begin to adequately express my gratitude because a few days earlier, I felt I was dying and the outcome was the opposite.

It's interesting to me that now, on two occasions, the first one being fourteen years ago when I got Lyme disease and had been dealing with some intestinal upset that started in Hawaii the previous year and which I had been unable to correct until I took the first antibiotic and suddenly all was fine. The taking of antibiotics have shifted me to a new place of health in a certain direction and somehow confirms that there is a time and place for everything.

What I Have Come to Know about Myself

I am a highly sensitive and sensual woman. I need to spend a large portion of my time in natural settings, apart from noisy neighbors, barking dogs, and where there is the least amount of disturbance from machinery. When I am away from my natural environment, I try to meditate on/around external stresses, finding gratitude for my senses and sensitivity. I can be stressed easily, and it takes me a long time to settle my energy after being out in the world and being social. I am intuitive, foresightful, appear calm on the outside but am nervous on the inside, generous, curious, caring, selfish from being sensitive, playful, empathic, capable, self-reliant, trusting, naive, passionate, occasionally wayward, persistent, compassionate, adventurous, and above all, grateful. I have a good sense of humor, laugh easily and spontaneously, and am quick witted. I am most content in and closest to nature, barefoot, and am unconventional in many ways. I choose not to wear any makeup or nail polish. I am unhurried and like to do things in my own time. I love being in my/a kitchen and the act/art of cooking, sharing my food, being cooked for, and above all, eating in silence.

"And in much of your talking, thinking is half-murdered—For thought is a bird of space, that in a cage of words may indeed unfold its wings but cannot fly" (*The Prophet* by Khalil Gibran).

I have discovered that everything, especially talking, is enhanced by my natural practice of not talking. Eating and walking in silence daily allows for full deep breathing and easy ability to hear the voice within—leaves space for all thoughts to flow in and out, in tune with my heart and breath, without interruption. The practice of yoga and meditation almost daily for forty-three years and my personal rituals serve as the foundation of my life, and out of it comes the greatest freedom. My small study of tai chi and aikido have also enhanced my life awareness.

My study and use of compass feng shui and the ancient 9 Star Ki cosmology system have helped/help to guide me in life decisions, move around the planet, and serve to better understand people and places. I prefer and strive to live off the grid, as sustainably as possible, and tread softly on the earth (though I enjoy city jaunts, especially if it's to be fed and entertained).

It suits me to be in warm, humid climates when I am able to be more relaxed and expanded, but I can adapt fairly easily to colder weather, especially when the woodstove is going at my cabin. Over the years, I have attended several very powerful, spiritually oriented workshops and seminars that have helped take me through various levels of healing and growth and to become more aware. I am on retreat most days that I am home or alone and enjoy the peace and calm that is at the core of my being. I love all creatures, great and small, and choose not to own any as pets, mainly for practical reasons. I am greatly fulfilled sharing/being of service to others and enjoy listening and sharing in a variety of ways. Mars was in Cancer and Venus was in Gemini on my birthdate, which aligns with a shamanic view. I am a seven metal rooster (7-5-7), and true to my nature, my mouth and feet are my greatest bodily sensors. I have a great love of fine fabrics and really enjoy getting dressed up!

I like to always have/make room for improvement and quietly strive to be a better person. Validation of self and therefore others is a fundamental part of my practice toward better health. I consider everything ingested to be food, always choosing the best, which includes occasionally enjoying premium sake or microbrewed beer and also, once in a blue moon, a few puffs of a hand-rolled, organic tobacco cigarette taken with respect and gratitude. I enjoy a variety of music, books, and films—including biographical, documentary, and fictional—and am in awe and in gratitude for all the work that goes into them.

Maybe it sounds like I have really got it together, but it's really just an ongoing process and work in progress! The truth is, as a very sensitive being, I have faced many shocking experiences from a young age and likely because of them, have been guided and inspired to change, move forward, and to love and know myself better. I avoid saying never or I believe too often, as it feels that the opposites are probably on the other side. I have strong intuition/telepathy in communicating with friends/people and usually am thinking about them just before they contact me or vice versa.

I am fully aware that the line is fine between my natural trait and tendency to be rather serious when trying to complete a task before being fully able to relax and my hypoglycemic tendency to go past the stopping point. It's quite easy these days to see myself inching into the red zone.

Everywhere I go, I do the cooking, primarily for myself because I know what fuels me best, but I am also so glad to have any opportunity to share it with others, knowing how beneficial it can be.

I enjoy allowing my spirit the freedom to move around on this planet and go where it needs to be and when service to others is requested.

These days, I always need to take a day or two off from the world in order to gather in and replenish my energy as I tend to get easily depleted. It's a challenge to be able to sufficiently relax to nourish myself when I have been out in the world in a social way, except, interestingly, when I take road trips or plane journeys alone. I usually only talk when necessary or move to do so in my own time. This is another natural trait that I learned about myself—that I function much better when I can do anything, including and especially talking, in my own time.

At this stage in my life, there is no doubt that I chose my parents/family in order that I would be triggered to wake up and become my essential authentic self.

Living a green life / staying connected to nature

All that I strive to do in my life is based on my connection to source/nature. I am dedicated to living in a sustainable way as much and more often as possible. I like to make use of available resources and am working toward leaving a smaller and smaller carbon footprint. I conserve water and electricity use, especially when I am at my cabin property, where I have my own well and solar system born out of the years before those luxuries were in place. I hand-wash clothes on a daily basis, compost all kitchen scraps, use scrap paper to light the woodstove, shop at thrift shops, and recycle anything I can. I also don't buy into the idea that we need a different soap to wash clothes and dishes.

I buy good-quality, unscented, concentrated laundry liquid, which doubles up as dishwashing liquid when watered down slightly. I have not ever owned a brand-new car, and my intention is for the next one to be a hybrid. I save up errands to be done and only drive out between one or three times a week.

I lean toward keeping a neutral acid/alkaline pH balance through the body rub; walking outside; eating an organic, plant-based, whole-foods diet; daily spiritual practice such as yoga, tai chi, and meditation; receiving supportive spiritual nurturing, such as acupuncture, shiatsu, lomi lomi, and reiki; and surrounding myself in all-natural clothing, bedding, and household furnishings. I hug a tree daily, giving thanks to the wood energy of my father and the soil energy of my mother for giving me life, and afterward, my whole being relaxes and my pace slows down. This is especially beneficial when I feel stressed or after traveling. When in an airport and there are any live plants, I will touch them to make and maintain my connection to the earth.

I use only all-natural, chemical-free, unscented household and personal/hair/body products. My senses are offended by the ghastly toxic smells of commercially scented detergents that are pouring into the atmosphere from the laundry machine vents. And when walking past people whose clothes reek of the smell, I am shocked again and again. But I am very aware that a diet that is overly stimulating and high in fats, animal, processed, sodium, sweeteners, chemically preserved, and artificially flavored and colored foods produces extreme behavior; very strong, unpleasant body odors; and sweating. The strong chemicals and scents that are used in commercial products are in an effort to help clean and mask these smells, and laundry machines seem to be running twenty-four hours a day every day. The more fats and salts in the diet, the more soaps and chemicals are used and therefore, the more water and usually some hot and therefore, more fuel is used to rinse off the soap. And then all this dirty water plus the chemicals/scents are going back into the earth and air, which is further contaminated.

The loud music many people insist on playing in their vehicles and in public places pummels my/our nervous systems and sends harmful vibrations into the atmosphere and earth. I wonder how the birds and creatures of the planet cope.

On occasion, I need to ingest antibiotics to assist in treating Lyme disease, and as it's almost impossible for me to swallow anything without chewing well, I empty out the antibiotics powder from the vivid, unnaturally colored capsules and mix/chew the contents in my mouth very well before swallowing. In this manner, I feel I am able to let my body know what's coming by tasting and chewing it and to produce more saliva to help alkalinize it before it enters my digestive system.

Humans are naturally hungry for spiritually satisfying, relaxing foods. Often, the food of choice has a tendency to have a short-lived, instant gratification without necessarily being balanced or complete with all the vital nutrients or healthy relaxants, which are needed more and more as life on the planet becomes ever more stressful.

I am also aware that we are very prone to being influenced and tempted in to try the latest fad food or diet along with being fed a lot of misinformation. I was one of these gullible people until I began to carefully apply the custom-made, balancing, modern-day macrobiotic diet and way of life that has kept me, for the most part, satisfied, confident, healthy, and endlessly grateful. I am convinced that if all peoples, especially students and adults, were educated in learning how to live and eat in a more balanced and strengthening way, parents would start having healthier pregnancies and to better nourish their children with the outcome being the reversal of all ill health. I feel strongly that if a macrobiotic lifestyle and plant-based diet were to be introduced into the prison systems, a huge shift would take place on so many levels.

As the years go by, the more I feed myself in this way, with plenty of variety and flare, the more intuitive I seem to be becoming about what my mind, body, and spirit desire. I seem to be guided to what is best in any given moment, rarely having cravings, curious for new tastes but not tempted into strange dietary or eating concepts. I realized many years ago that once I found what my mind body and spirit were asking for, needed, I was no longer hungry. I now simply listen to my inner voice and observe from this peaceful, calm place of knowing.

"Dis-moi ce que tu manges, je te dirai ce que tu es."

"Tell me what you eat, and I will tell you what you are" (*The Physiology of Taste: Meditations on Transcendental Gastronomy* by Jean Anthelme Brillat-Savarin).

There is so much sickness and disease on the planet both in humans and animals (who for the most part are fed foods that are prepared in a similar method to the foods that humans consume and which are directly responsible for causing the same imbalances that are in our bodies and minds) that is likely manifested from our ever-increasing departure from staying close with and supporting nature.

We are bombarded and are bombarding ourselves morning, noon, and night with so much pollution and toxins that all living beings, creatures, and plant life are struggling to keep a healthy balance. It seems sensible to try and lessen both the intake and buildup of excess and protect ourselves from their harmful effects by strengthening our health with highest quality of organic whole foods, liquids, and natural environments. Humans have a brilliant built-in protection in the form of mucus, which is very alkalinizing and is produced to help alkalize and/or surround anything extreme or harmful that enters our system. When there is an excess, the body has to produce so much protective mucus that there is a buildup that becomes stagnant. We call this an infection.

It is my understanding that ancient civilizations discovered the amazing energetic value of everything—particularly each and every food and beverage and in specific combinations. I have been consciously incorporating certain special remedy drinks, dishes, and activities to help relax, soften, draw out, and naturally eliminate past excesses stored deep in and around my body and organs. And there is little doubt that it has and continues to bring about the desired outcome and effects. I feel lighter, more confident, balanced, happier, and with a brighter view of life and the future.

After all, we are and become what we eat.

In a nutshell

I have had an active macrobiotic practice for the past thirty-two years, either cooking for Denny's clients referred to me by him or through word of mouth, including many cancer cases and a few with eating disorders. I have hosted and attended many monthly potlucks in Upstate New York, started a wholesale macro-food buying club, given small presentations of my story, offered cooking class series both in New York and Hawaii, done some private cooking, and given several hypoglycemia and 9 Star Ki presentations, the most recent I called *The Aah of Eating* at the Temple of Peace in Haiku, Maui, Hawaii.

When giving a consultation, I want to know about the person and will get them started with the basic format. If they have a difficult or serious condition, then I steer them to Denny and when possible, will attend the consultation with them in order to better interpret his recommendations. The purpose is self-empowerment, something often difficult for people who are used to eating out and being dependent on others/outside help. I offer them the simple lifestyle guidelines and encourage them to take full responsibility for their health. Having the tools to help shape our destiny is a great and wonderful gift and once applied, boosts confidence in our ability to take care of and to become more and more our essential healthy selves.

The most profoundly significant days/events of my life that I can recall include:

The day my father left our family.
The day I went to boarding school.
The birthday of my daughter.
Practicing hatha yoga.
Moving to the United States of America.
Eating consciously for the first time.
First consultation with Denny Waxman.
Purchase of land in Ulster County, New York.
Building my cabin.
Discovering Hawaii.
Miscarriage.
My mother's death.
Finishing this book!

My understanding of hypoglycemia in relation
to eating disorders and addiction

All living things are dependent on food, water, and air to sustain life energy. In good health, we (would) naturally/intuitively nourish ourselves at regular times with appropriate foods and liquids, according to the inner body clock and circadian rhythm. The inner organs all have specific times of day and/or night when they are most active or inactive, and they send a message to the brain to pay attention. Our ancestors lived in this way, eating, sleeping, and waking according to their inner clocks that in turn were in alignment with the rest of the planet: waking at first light, eating regular meals, always at the same hour, working hard, playing, and retiring to sleep early. Since the onset of highly refined and processed foods, we humans have been getting further away from our naturally healthy living styles and cycles.

Skipping meals has become the norm as caffeine, sugar, and other sweet-laden beverages replace breakfast and/or lunch and bypass the real hunger messages. On the extreme side of this are those who are starting their days with large plates of heavy animal foods and sweet pastries. All these food choices have begun to take their toll on the function of the spleen and insulin production of the pancreas. Insulin is a hormone made by the pancreas that allows our body to use sugar (glucose) from carbohydrates in the food that we eat for energy or to store glucose for future use. Insulin helps keeps our blood sugar level from getting too high (hyperglycemia) or too low (hypoglycemia) and is probably one of the most important ingredients in sustaining life in humans.

People with eating disorders have poorly functioning, compromised spleen and pancreas activity. For example, the pancreas of a person with anorexic tendency is probably not producing enough insulin to feed the blood and therefore brain with sufficient sugars for clear, healthy thinking and life action. This person will have what I call a tight condition, and if the organs are sending messages to our brain, then the mind will in turn think tightly. I have not heard anyone outside the macrobiotic teachings actually make any mention or correlation of the internal organs in this way.

In fact, it is generally thought that a person with anorexia is forcing him or herself to not eat; hence, the term anorexia nervosa. I see it very differently. It is the pancreatic/spleen condition that creates the tight mindedness. For after all, it is the most natural and healthy instinct to survive and nourish ourselves when hungry. A body, mind, and spirit that is nourished, relaxed, and happy in all ways will rarely be influenced through the mind not to eat when hungry. Of course, any external upset, including physical and/or psychological, will naturally affect the sensitivity of any living being, animals, and humans alike, and at these times, we are triggered to a different place of survival, including forfeiting food, even if it is time to eat. At times of great stress, the inner organs can be easily shocked and will contract quickly. Then the vicious cycle becomes more complex. A baby that would not or could not eat at birth (as in my case) is hardly making a mindful decision to not eat. Rather, its condition is influencing its behavior.

Bulimia is almost the opposite of anorexia in that a person becomes so hungry from not eating/skipping meals that they overeat, and generally, the food choices become increasingly extreme.

This flood of, usually, excess extreme food into the system initially makes the person feel happy but unable to stop, then overloads and stresses the organs and speaking from experience, triggers a need to get empty again because of the great discomfort experienced. Hence, the bulimic person being attracted to purging either through use of laxatives or inducing vomiting.

I have come to understand that anorexia, bulimia, obesity, and addiction are all symptoms of the underlying condition of hypoglycemia. If the pancreatic/spleen function and insulin production/secretion is addressed by nourishing the person appropriately with glucose-forming foods, these organs will begin to heal and start to produce the right quantity and quality of insulin for good health.

This is Webster's definition of hypoglycemia:

> A below normal concentration of glucose in the bloodstream. Glucose, the body's chief source of energy, is essential for all vital activity from day-dreaming (brain/thinking activity) to ditch-digging (physical activity).
>
> Symptoms: The severity of the symptoms of hypoglycemia depends on how fast and how low the glucose level in the blood falls. Some symptoms are associated with a rapid fall in glucose level, which activates the autonomic nervous system and triggers the release of the 'emergency' hormone epinephrine (adrenalin). These symptoms may include weakness, shakiness, rapid heartbeat, anxiety, hunger and nausea. Other symptoms, associated with a slow fall in glucose level or with prolonged or severe hypoglycemia, result from a shortage of glucose in the brain. These symptoms may include headache, lethargy, faintness, visual disturbances and even convulsions. Repeated severe episodes of hypoglycemia may cause permanent brain damage.

Causes. Hypoglycemia can be induced by any condition that causes glucose to be added to the bloodstream more slowly than it is removed. A condition that persists or recurs is generally a symptom of physical or emotional malfunction. Hypoglycemia is most often caused by disorders that result in hyperinsulinism, (the excessive secretion of insulin by the pancreas). The excessive insulin acts to reduce the glucose level in the blood below its normal range.

Functions of the spleen and pancreas

The spleen and pancreas are primarily responsible for the digestion and distribution of food and nutrients.

Spleen:
- filters out foreign organisms that may infect the blood;
- removes old or damaged platelets and red blood cells;
- stores extra blood and releases it as needed; and
- forms some types of white blood cells.

In ancient times, the spleen was considered to be the seat of emotions. Today, the overemotional person is pointing to an imbalance in this organ.

Pancreas:
- secretes pancreatic juices into the duodenum/small intestine; and
- secretes insulin, glucagon, and somatostatin into the bloodstream.

The health of the pancreas determines the quality and strength of the enzymes it secretes, which in turn largely determines how well nutrients are absorbed through the small intestine.

Because the spleen and pancreas work very closely together in the human body and play a vital and key part in our general well-being, a contraction in either or both of these two organs, which causes much disruption in the flow of energy, is a common symptom in people with hypoglycemia. Certain foods eventually cause and then exacerbate the condition so that this vicious cycle tends to get us stuck in a self-destructive pattern of behavior that comes from the tightness in these organs. The mind therefore registers tight, and we become more tight, controlling, and into ourselves.

Hypoglycemia, or low blood sugar (glucose), often develops from the same kind of dietary extremes that causes diabetes, but instead of a diabetic shortage of insulin, an excess is produced. In time, if insulin overproduction continues, the pancreas becomes overworked and loses its ability to produce sufficient and/or effective insulin, the result being diabetes. This is why hypoglycemia often precedes the onset of diabetes.

The pathological symptoms of hypoglycemia are many, and I would even go as far as to say that all disease in man/womankind today is surely linked to this low blood sugar problem.

The following is a list of these symptoms, which includes many that are commonly found in medical texts:

alcohol dependency;
blurred vision;
bulimia;
cold hands and feet;
constant hunger;
cool, wet skin;
cravings for sweets;
crying spells;
depression;
distorted judgment;
dizziness;
drowsiness;
drug dependency (recreational and pharmaceutical);
dry or burning mouth;
eye ache;
fluttering feeling in the chest;
fast pulse;
fatigue;

headaches;
hot flashes;
hyperactivity;
impotence;
inability to eat/anorexia;
insomnia;
irritability;
lack of concentration/attention deficit disorder;
loss of appetite;
loss of sex drive;
low blood pressure;
mental disturbances;
muscle pain or cramps;
noise or light sensitivity;
numbness, especially in the mouth;
pale skin;
ringing in the ears;
shortness of breath;
sweating;
swollen feet;
temper tantrums;
weakness in the legs; and
worry, anxiety

The physiological and behavioral symptoms connected with hypoglycemia can often be overlooked/disassociated (note that I have listed anorexia, bulimia, and drug dependency in both categories):

anorexia;
bulimia;
coveting;
collecting large quantities of objects/things/artifacts, which are often, though not always, of the same nature;
drug dependency;
sneaky, secretive behavior; and
stealing.

"When hungry eat: when tired sleep." [Zen Buddhist saying]

(This concept was given by a Zen master as an example of being enlightened or free. However, I have lately been wondering if this particular master had hypoglycemia and being spiritually inclined, had found a way to use his condition as another tool to practice not being attached.)

There are many schools of thought about the best way to cure hypoglycemia.

A high-protein diet has been considered one of the most popular ones because protein digests slowly, supplies energy gradually, and does not trigger excess insulin production. But a high-protein diet, which is lacking in the vital sugar (glucose) necessary to help insulin production, eventually often causes and presents other serious health problems.

In my experience, I would suggest that the principal remedy for hypoglycemia is the application of a regulated lifestyle and a balanced, whole-food, plant-based diet that is rich in complex carbohydrates in their whole forms. Grains, vegetables, beans, and pulses, like animal proteins, take time to break down and metabolize and also contain nutrients that regulate insulin production. Eating small meals at regular times daily in a calm, unhurried manner; thoroughly chewing all food; eating balanced meals; and not mixing different dishes on the plate can all assist in the healing process and help regulate the spleen and pancreas function. Minimizing or avoiding denatured and refined foods is helpful because these foods lack the minerals and other nutrients, which control all metabolic activities, including insulin production.

Refined flour or sugar, for example, are composed primarily of carbohydrates that deliver energy and warmth. The protein, bran, and minerals and hence, the main nutrients that are refined away would have been incorporated into the blood, hormones, and various body fluids to cool, moisten, and subdue the burning of sugars into energy. The hypoglycemic body robs its own tissues of these needed nutrients, thereby losing the deep controlling reserves that stabilize it during dietary extremes and stress in general. Thus, those with low blood sugar (glucose) may notice fluctuations in blood sugar levels according to what was eaten at the last meal.

Many people who decide to restrict grains or gluten intake can often become tight and set up cravings for wanting extremes. The gluten-free fad is depriving those folk of vital relaxing *yin* grains and flour/bread. Good quality sourdough bread is a vitally important nourishing and relaxing food as it contains important enzymes, B vitamins, and probiotics.

Those who start the day on strong coffee, sweet pastries, choc-olate, and/or skip meals will often be drawn to do more of the same and will be needing supplements and/or ending the day with a large, extremely rich, salty meal.

A few adjustments would be made for those either overweight or underweight (i.e., more or less oil, bread, pasta, and fatty foods—like nuts, beans, and seeds). Salt and salty products needs to be used sparingly because it reduces blood sugar. Seaweeds, on the other hand, which have a salty flavor, are useful in moderation because of their rich protein and mineral content. Toasted nori seaweed is the one exception, which can be used as a daily snack. It helps to reduce cravings for salty, crispy snacks and has added bonus of helping pro-tect against radiation pollution. People with hypoglycemia are gener-ally not only mineral deficient but also usually lack adequate essential fatty acids (EFAs). This often manifests in one or more of these signs: dry hair and skin, low body weight, poor glandular function (espe-cially of the pancreas and the adrenals), and liver / gall-bladder-re-lated imbalances, such as irritability, depression, nervousness, pains, and cramps.

The hypoglycemic personality

The hypoglycemic person often has a long history of sugar abuse from young age and is often drawn to sugar in adulthood in an attempt to placate some deep, underlying emotional disharmony.

Hypoglycemia in its turn eventually causes its own set of problems. The brain needs adequate good-quality blood sugar at all times to function properly, so blood sugar lows affects the mental process. With insufficient sugar for the brain cells, the hypoglycemic person can develop foggy concepts or distorted moral senses. In children, lack of blood sugar can lead to retardation and is often related to juvenile delinquency. Alcoholism, based on the overconsumption of sugar in the form of alcohol, nearly always has hypoglycemic symptoms. Low blood sugar is also present in people with disorders such as schizophrenia, drug addiction, and obesity. All merely symptoms of the underlying root condition.

It is clear to me that one of the major factors in excessive sugar consumption is the quantity of meat (and most animal food) consumption. Too much meat in the diet causes sugar cravings as an attempt to establish a protein/carbohydrate balance. It is also known that excessive meat eating generates prostaglandins that cause pain, inflammation, and depression and that sugar and alcohol can temporarily reduce these symptoms. Overcoming such a hypoglycemic cycle often requires fresh insights and inspiration to change. Oftentimes, these insights and changes are propelled through a severe illness or accident, which tends to open us up to change.

I recommend highly the reading of two books that may help those seeking to better understand and implement all that I have mentioned so far.

The China Study by Dr. Colin Campbell PhD and *The Ultimate Guide to Eating for Longevity* by Denny Waxman.

Underneath is a list of the steps that I used and now recommend to help in recovery of hypoglycemia and for all who wish to attain a great level of health and well-being.

Steps to recovery

Introduce, gradually, a wide variety of whole foods prepared in ways that soften and relax. As the body begins to relax, so, too, does the mind, and we then start to make wiser choices.

Set and have regular mealtimes every day to help regulate the production and output of insulin and glucose.

Sit down for all meals, including snacks.

Avoid extra distractions that are not related to eating—i.e., TV, cell phones, books, and other electronics. I strongly suggest that phones are switched off to avoid temptation to answer.

Chew all food until it is liquid. Thirty-two teeth connect to thirty-two vertebrae and twelve organs, and stimulation from chewing soothes and calms the entire central nervous system along with alkalinizing all food before it enters the stomach.

Giving thanks/saying prayers before eating also helps to calm and align with the act of nourishing ourselves.

Eat one or two bowls of vegetable soup daily.

Always include at least one grain and one vegetable at each meal to create balance.

Wait at least two, preferably three, hours after eating evening meal before going to bed. It is best to have an empty stomach so that the body and organs can rest and repair.

Do a daily body rub with hot water and 100 percent cotton wash/facecloth. This can be done before or after a shower or bath but not at the same time.

Walk half an hour daily outside to help create balance and harmony and to align with the pulse of the planet. Walking barefoot on dewy grass or along the beach or in the woods is especially alkalinizing and has a very restorative effect.

Wear 100 percent cotton clothing next to the skin. This has the most alkalinizing/neutralizing energetic effect.

Try and duplicate nature in the home by installing wood floors, using all-natural products and fabrics, and keeping green, oxygen-giving plants in every room. Again, this all helps keep us more aligned and alkaline.

Keep home clean and orderly as much as possible.

Switch to gas/propane for cooking, which has a calmer energy and is also more alkalinizing. Minimize use of electric gadgets and switch them off.

Spend time each day in personal spiritual exercise and ritual—i.e., yoga, meditation, aikido, tai chi. This helps move stagnation, open the meridians/chakras, and align with spirit/source.

Take time for relaxation, hobbies, creative pursuits, and outdoor activities—such as gardening, fishing. All are harmonizing/balancing.

Try and find a sense of adventure in all that we do.

Nurture appreciation and gratitude for all.

When suggesting any changes to a loved one or friend, it's always best to offer some new things to add to their current diet rather than telling them to stop eating certain foods. The more healthy and balanced foods we ingest, the more we will crave those and the less we will desire the others.

If blood sugar becomes low in between meals, a mildly sweet-tasting drink, carrot juice combination, or a few unsalted nuts or seeds can usually do the trick to top it up.

If any meal is not properly balanced, there will still be hunger and that is when there will be cravings for snacks and sweets.

I honestly think that the reason so many humans suffer from eating disorders, addiction, and unhappiness within themselves and their lives is because their spirits are searching for and have yet to find the right support and nourishment. A macrobiotic lifestyle and a food plan custom made to suit each individual condition can support (our) spiritual life in a/the most profound way.

Parents and guardians of symptomatic and highly sensitive children can give the greatest support by creating a more gentle, unhurried, and peaceful environment around and during mealtimes.

Playing some beautiful, relaxing, and/or classical music along with plenty of hugs, daily reassurance of love, massage, and touch can all be very soothing and nurturing to the child's nervous system and are vitally important in the healing process. Highly sensitive children with eating disorders and/or addiction often are trying to tell their parents that the environment they are living in does not support their basic, natural needs.

Never say never

We set ourselves up for disaster by saying, "I will never do this or that again." Better to add new things or ways of being and doing, which in turn leave less room for the old stuff/ways.

Truth, Reconciliation, and Restoration

If we don't have a conscience of wrongdoing, we don't have a conscience of shame and we don't/can't have empathy or ability take responsibility and to do the right and moral thing to put things to right. Forgiveness takes a moment to enact.

Know and Love Ourselves

Take time to listen to the inner voice.

Feel gratitude for all we have, especially our life and the parents who gave us a chance to be here.

Give ourselves the best in all that we choose to eat and do, no matter what it is.

Use our sensitivity to guide us.

"The heart of the home beats in the kitchen and a healthy one beats three times a day" (excerpt from *The Great Pearl of Wisdom* by Bangambiki Habyarimana).

Making art in my kitchen

I see my kitchen as my art studio, and my larder, pantry, and refrigerator are my art/paint palettes from which I spontaneously choose my colors/food in order to create the day's cooking/dishes.

The ideas just come to me based on any number of things (i.e., what ingredients I have and what was eaten the day before), and I rarely question the inner voice, though sometimes will debate/consider one or other choice that comes to mind, especially when I am cooking for others.

In order to feel free to follow through on these choices, I make sure I have as many variety of all food categories as is possible along with plenty of supplemental seasonings and items.

Organically grown grains, beans, seaweeds, flours, root, ground, round and leafy green vegetables, some fruits, seeds, nuts, tempeh, tofu, seitan, natto, dried and cured foods, such as tempeh, tofu, natto, umeboshi, and a variety of misos and pickles, sourdough bread and tortillas, apple juice, soy and almond milk, microbrew beers, sake, and single-malt whiskey are all included.

I also like to have a variety of good-quality, vegan, prepared foods, such as Amy's low-sodium canned soups (barley, split pea, lentil, no-chicken noodle) and potpies, plant-based burgers, and burritos.

This is probably one of the more challenging tasks in this section of the book, as I am one of those people who, after forty-six years of playing with food, nowadays rarely follow any recipe to the t. I can eyeball amounts and am cooking intuitively. So coming up with accurate ingredient amounts taxes my brain!

In addition, my cup and spoon measurements are usually parts—i.e., a cup is often a handy mug or glass and a teaspoon or tablespoon, whatever is at hand. Because I travel in and out of a variety of different climates, I am constantly adjusting the amount of liquid, oil, and seasonings. The exceptions are when I am cooking for a person under Denny's recommendations, and when I have discovered a recipe that sounds interesting, I might follow the guidelines the first time.

Coming from a place of near starvation and self-deprivation, nowadays, I prefer to be able to cook and eat with joy and (reckless) abandon. There are certain foods that I cannot tolerate so easily. Refined sugar, other tropical sweeteners, and caffeine seem to catch up with me.

The high and then low of these very stimulating foods play havoc with my adrenals, so I generally avoid them. But I also like to be able to offer guests various things that they are used to having, so even though I don't use them, having, for example, some organic coffee and honey on hand, can be helpful in making them feel more comfortable.

I use a lot of sweet root and round vegetables in my cooking, and I especially love onions. (I was once nicknamed the queen of root vegetables at a workshop in Oregon.) They all seem to keep me feeling grounded and happy, and they support good pancreas and spleen function and the production of good-quality insulin.

I eat some type/style of whole-grain brown rice or rice product each day, sometimes twice. If I don't, it feels like something is missing, my spirit cannot settle, and sleep evades me.

I make sure that I have food ready cooked/prepared to simply warm up on days that I have been out in the world. This prevents me from becoming more yang (my tendency) and ensures a more relaxed meal and all-around life experience of caring for myself.

The acts of buying, cooking, and sharing of my food is a very important part of my life journey, and the idea of not doing any part of this sustainable practice seems foreign and unimaginable. Something feels especially not balanced during the week if I haven't invited a friend to share lunch or at least brought some freshly made soup or amazake to share.

My macrobiotic mentors and dear friends, Harry Hart and Loretta Quartey, shared an interesting concept, which I have come to favor along the way. Their idea was simply this: If we get too fussy about eating only organic, which can restrict/limit wider variety of ingredients and are obsessed about cleanliness, our immune system could be spoiled, which would in turn make us more sensitive and prone to greater risks of contamination / side effects / illness. When I am traveling, it's sometimes not possible to get organically grown foods, spring water, or be able shower or bathe. So with the understanding that variety is important, I will buy nonorganic produce. For example, fresh watercress is such a delicious and important green vegetable that I will gladly buy it anytime available.

Fifteen of Some of My Favorite Recipes

Satisfying shoyu soup

Ingredients:
2 inch piece kombu seaweed
1/3 daikon or 1 small turnip sliced very thinly and in half-moons
1 small or 1/2 medium onion sliced thinly in 1/2 moons
2 dried shiitake mushrooms
2 slices of tofu cut into small 1/4-inch cubes
1 large or 3 small tender green leaves thinly sliced (choose from daikon, kale, mustard greens, collards)
8 cups water
sea salt
5 to 7 teaspoons of shoyu
thinly sliced scallions for garnish
optional: 3 pieces of fried mochi 1 inch squares or cooked pasta or noodles

Preparation:
Place water, kombu, and shiitake plus soaking water in a pot and bring to boil covered. Cook for 2 to 3 minutes.
Remove the Kombu and set aside for future use.
Remove shiitake, slice thinly, and return to pot.
Add the onions and cook for a minute.
Add small-pinch salt.
Add the daikon or turnip and continue to cook for 5 minutes.
Add the tofu cubes and another pinch salt.
Add the greens and simmer for 2 minutes.
Add shoyu and simmer for 2 minutes.

If using mochi, cut into bite-size pieces, use a little sesame oil, and either fry in cast-iron pan or deep-fry in safflower oil until golden and puffed.

Place 3 pieces of mochi or cooked pasta/noodles in each bowl and a small amount of scallion garnish and ladle the hot broth over the top.

Pureed broccoli, onion, and jinenjo soup

Jinenjo, also called yama or nama imo, is a variety of wild (yama) or cultivated (nama) Japanese mountain yam and has a very powerfully strong energy. Therefore, I use it sparingly, mostly in puréed, creamy-style soups or winter warming stews. It is regularly imported from Japan and can be bought at various Japanese markets in the United States of America.

Serves 4 to 6.

Ingredients:
1 large crown of broccoli, washed—peel the fibrous outer layer and chop the stalks and tops into small cubes
2 medium onions, peeled and chopped into cubes
4 inch piece of jinenjo (Japanese mountain yam), peeled and cut into cubes
4 cups water
1/4 teaspoon sea salt
3 to 5 drops of shoyu or tamari
fresh or toasted nori seaweed for garnish

Preparation:
Put the water, onions, and jinenjo into a pot.
Add 1/4 teaspoon of salt and bring to a boil and simmer for 15 minutes with lid on.
Add the broccoli stalks, tops, and the rest of the salt and simmer for another 5 minutes.
Blend straight away and return to pot.
Add shoyu or tamari and simmer for 1 minute.

Serve with either freshly chopped or whole, fried parsley or small pieces of torn-up, toasted nori seaweed.

For variety, substitute the broccoli with either hard winter squash, rutabagas leeks, cauliflower, and/or parsnips.

Hearty breakfast porridge

Ingredients:
3/4 cup short- or medium-grain brown rice or combination of both
1/8 cup raw or toasted buckwheat groats
1/8 cup green lentils (or French lentils, azuki, split peas, or mung beans)—sometimes I will put in precooked beans toward end of cooking
a sprinkle of whole, pearled, or wild barley (or medium-brown rice, farro, whole or cracked oat groats)
5 cups filtered water
pinch sea salt or 1/2 inch kombu seaweed

Preparation:
Rinse and soak the grain/bean mixture in the water for a minimum of 4 hours. (I usually do this after breakfast.)
Bring to a boil, add the salt, and simmer for 2 to 3 hours. (I usually do this after supper and then its ready to warm up for breakfast the following morning.)
NB. I sometimes use a wide-mouthed, stainless-steel food thermos when needing to conserve fuel and/or on a road trip. After bringing the grain/bean mixture to a boil, I simmer for 1/2 to 1 hour, pour the hot cereal into the thermos, and seal. In the morning, it's ready to serve. For an even creamier porridge, I will cook it for another 1/2 hour. Yum.
Serve with roasted ground sesame seeds, whole roasted pumpkin seeds, or anything else you like, including any savory condiment if desired.

Boiled coarsely ground brown rice cereal with corn grits, quick-cook oats, or tabouli

Ingredients:
3/4 cup ground medium- or short-grain brown rice
1/4 cup yellow or white corn grits, Scottish-style oats, or cracked wheat
3 to 4 cups of water
good pinch of sea salt
optional: olive oil drizzled over hot cereal at end of cooking for richer taste

Preparation:
Soak the grains in the water. Use more water for breakfast time.
Bring to a boil using a wire whisk to prevent lumping until cereal begins to thicken.
Add salt, turn flame down, and cook gently with lid on for 30 to 40 minutes, stirring occasionally to cook evenly.
Drizzle a little olive oil over cereal if desired.
Serve with any condiment you like.

Nishime (my all-time favorite, most delicious, simple Japanese root vegetable dish)

Ingredients:
1 inch square of kombu or sea kelp, rinsed or soaked
1/8 teaspoon sea salt
1/8 teaspoon shoyu or tamari
water to cover the bottom of the pot
3 cups of a variety of root and round vegetables, washed and cut into bite-size chunks
hearty-style greens—such as celery, cabbage, or leeks—can also be used and occasionally shiitake mushrooms and fresh tofu or tempeh for a richer dish
Serves 6.

Preparation:

Place water and kombu or kelp, cut into thin slices, in bottom of heavy pot.

Layer each vegetable, adding a tiny pinch of salt in between, and bring to boil.

Simmer with lid on for 20 to 40 minutes depending on preference.

Add the shoyu or tamari, and with the lid back on, gently shake the pot to blend in the seasoning and simmer for 2 more minutes.

Suggestions for veggie combinations:

turnip, kabocha squash, onion, kombu

carrot, leeks, kombu

daikon, onion, yellow summer squash or winter squash, kombu

daikon, jinenjo, cabbage, kombu

kabocha squash, onion, kombu, tofu

carrot, sweet potato, onion, kombu, optional tofu

turnip, shiitake mushroom, kombu

carrot, celery, hard winter squash, kombu

Pressure-cooked, braised onions

Ingredients:

3 pounds sweet or Vidalia onions

1 cup of water

1/4 teaspoon of sea salt

1 teaspoon of sesame oil (optional and sometimes I use corn or soybean oil)

Preparation:

Peel and cut onions in 1/2 and place in pressure cooker with water.

Seal lid, bring to pressure, and then cook for 15 minutes.

Once the pressure is down, remove lid and continue to cook on medium-high heat to cook off most of the excess liquid, which can take up to 20 minutes.

Add the salt toward the end and then the oil.

These onions are, quite simply, delicious and give a happy feeling. They can be served with tempeh, fish, and tofu.

Rutabaga or purple daikon and onion kinpira

This is modern sweet version of a Japanese dish that traditionally uses burdock and carrots. A couple of years ago, when it was difficult finding turnips on Maui, I experimented using purple daikon and it was so rich and delicious that I have added it to my favorites list.

Ingredients:
1 medium rutabaga or purple daikon
2 medium to large onions
golden, untoasted sesame oil
water to cover
sea salt
a few drops of shoyu, natural soy sauce
freshly grated and squeezed ginger juice

Preparation:
Wash and trim the root vegetable and slice thinly into matchsticks.

Peel and thinly slice the onions into half-moons.

Coat cast-iron frying pan with sesame oil and bring up to medium heat.

Add onions and cook until glazed. Add a pinch of salt.

Add sliced root vegetable onto and add water to cover.

Bring up to boil, turn the heat down, and cover.

Cook on medium heat until most liquid is cooked off.

Add shoyu and cook uncovered until all liquid has cooked off.

Add freshly squeezed ginger juice and gently mix in.

Chickpea stew (option with fried tofu)

Ingredients:
1 cup chickpeas, washed and soaked overnight for 8 hours
1-inch kombu
2 small onions
2 carrots
1 large stick celery
1 large bay leaf
1/4 teaspoon of sea salt
optional: 1 cup fried tofu cubes
4 cups filtered water

In summer months, I sometimes add yellow summer squash and/or some large cubes of pre-fried, fresh tofu to the vegetables for a lighter dish.

In winter months, I might add a little jinenjo and/or fried seitan or seitan loaf or sausages for a richer, more warming dish.

Preparation:
Drain off the chickpeas in soaking water and rinse.
Place wiped kombu in bottom of pressure cooker and chickpeas on top.
Add enough water to cover plus 2 inches extra.
Bring to boil with lid off and scoop off any foam.
Put lid on, seal, and bring to pressure, then turn down flame to cook for 50 minutes.
Meanwhile, wash and cut all the vegetables and place in another large pot with the bay leaf.
If you are pressed for time, add water to cover and cook with lid on for 20 minutes.
When the chickpeas have cooked and pressure has come down, add chickpeas to the vegetables.
Continue cooking with lid off to cook off any excess liquid, as this dish should be too soupy (though leftovers can be made into a delicious soup or added to miso soup for richness).
Season with salt.

I usually make double this quantity, fill mason jars, seal, and/or allow some to cool and freeze individual 4-ounce and 8-ounce plastic food containers for travel and emergency food supply.

Quick sauté onions with fresh dandelion greens or arugula, fresh shiitake, and tofu

Ingredients:
1 small white or red onion, sliced in 1/4-inch-thick half-moons
3 to 5 fresh shiitake mushrooms, gently cleaned, cut into 1/8-inch slices
8 ounce fresh baby arugula, washed and drained
4 ounce fresh tofu, crumbled
1/4 teaspoon sea salt
1/2 teaspoon ume vinegar
1 teaspoon light sesame or olive oil
1/4 cup of water
a few drops of mirin
Serves 4 to 5.

Preparation:
Gently heat oil in a stainless-steel frying pan or wok.
Add the onions and a small pinch of the salt and briskly sauté on medium flame for 10 seconds.
Add the shiitake and another pinch of salt and sauté for 5 seconds.
Add the yellow squash and a pinch of salt and sauté 10 seconds.
Add the crumbled tofu and ume vinegar and gently sauté for 2 seconds.
Add the arugula and water and gently blend all the ingredients.
Simmer while continuing to blend for about a minute.
Sprinkle in a few drops of mirin.
Turn onto a big platter immediately and spread out to help quickly cool.
Use a variety of vegetables each time you make this to give the greatest benefits and pleasure.

Napa cabbage / tempeh wraps

Ingredients:
1/2 pound of authentic fresh or prefrozen tempeh sliced into five-by-one-inch sticks
2 tablespoon of safflower oil
5 washed napa cabbage leaves
water
2 tablespoon shoyu
5 thin ginger slices
1 teaspoon mirin
sea salt
1 heaped teaspoon kuzu powder
toothpicks

Preparation:
Using a cast-iron pan, fry slices of tempeh in the oil until golden brown on both sides.

Add water to cover, ginger slices, shoyu, and mirin and bring to boil.

Turn down heat and cook covered until 3/4 liquid is cooked off.

Remove the tempeh and put onto a plate to cool. Discard the ginger slices.

Meanwhile, in a large frying pan, steam the whole napa leaves in a little water with a tiny pinch of salt for 1 minute.

Place onto a platter to cool.

Pour the cooking water into a bowl to cool.

Wrap each slice of tempeh in a napa leaf starting at the base of the leaf. Secure with a toothpick.

Put the wraps back into the cast-iron pan with its cooking liquid and cook for 2 to 3 minutes.

Using the nappe cooking water, add the kuzu powder and mix until dissolved.

Extract the cooking liquid from the tempeh wraps and blend in with kudzu.

Add the mixture back to the pan and bring to a simmer for a minute.

Place wraps in a serving dish and pour the kuzu sauce over the top.

Fried fish with scallions and sweet miso sauce

Ingredients:
Any desirable fresh or frozen white-meat fish, such as snapper, flounder, bass, grouper, perch
5 scallions cleaned and sliced thinly on the diagonal
olive or safflower oil
sweet white miso mixed with a little English yellow mustard or wasabi (mix powder with a little water to make a smooth paste)
2 tablespoon sake or mirin
lemon wedges

Preparation:
Spread a generous amount of the miso/mustard paste on the top side of each piece fish.
Bring oil to medium heat in cast-iron pan and gently fry the scallions, top side first, and remove from pan onto serving plate.
Fry the fish on both sides and remove from the pan.
Add the mirin or sake to the pan and stir to blend with the cooking juices.
Arrange fish on the serving plate and use a fork to place a layer of the scallions on top and spoon the sauce on it all.
Place lemon wedges around plate.

Cucumber / shallot / daikon sprouts / tofu salad

Ingredients:
1 seedless cucumber, gently wiped with cotton kitchen towel (English hothouse or Japanese varieties are my favorites)
1 baby shallot
a handful of daikon sprouts

a pinch of sea salt

1/2 block of tofu, rinsed and covered in a dry cotton towel to remove excess water

2 tablespoon ume plum vinegar

Preparation:

Slice the tofu in 1/4 pieces and lay flat separately on a plate.

Dribble the ume vinegar over the tofu, turning to coat both sides, and let it sit.

Score the surface of the cucumber with a fork from top to bottom, slice in half lengthways, then in very thin half-moons, and place in a large bowl.

Peel and slice the shallot in wafer-thin slices and add to cucumbers.

Using hands, gently mix in the sea salt.

Crumble the tofu and gently fold into the cucumbers along with the daikon greens.

Blanched bok choy, watercress, scallion, and sunflower seed salad

Ingredients:

1 head bok choy, washed and sliced on the diagonal in 1/2-inch cuts

good amount of fresh watercress, rinsed and thick stalks cut

3 large scallions, rinsed and sliced on the diagonal in 1/4-inch cuts

1/4 cup of raw sunflower seeds, rinsed

ume vinegar

4 cups of water

a tiny pinch of sea salt

Preparation:

Bring the water to a boil and add the salt.

Systematically blanch each of the vegetables separately for about 1 minute, scooping them out onto a new clean plate to cool down most quickly.

It's important to keep bringing the water back to a boil before adding the next vegetable variety but making sure not to actually let the water boil while the vegetables are in the pot

Start with the least-strong flavor, being the bok choy, then the watercress and then the scallions.

Finally, add the sunflower seeds to newly boiling water, and these can actually boil for a minute.

Allow all to cool before mixing gently in a beautiful salad bowl. Scoop out about 4 to 5 tablespoons of the blanching water into a cup, add a few drops of ume vinegar, and sprinkle over the salad.

NB. I will sometimes use the blanching water as a base for making sweet vegetable soup or for cooking pasta or noodles.

This is a very useful and important water- and fuel-saving method/tip that I have adopted in times of need. Other times, the water can be cooled and used to water plants or vegetables in the house and garden.

Poached pears in kuzu / rice syrup sauce with maple-almond cream

Ingredients:
4 pears
1 1/2 cup of water
1 to 2 tablespoons of rice syrup
1 tablespoons of kuzu root
a tiny pinch of sea salt
cinnamon
fresh mint to garnish
Serves 4 to 6.

Preparation:
Gently wash pears, peel (or not), cut in 1/2, and scoop out the seeds with a teaspoon. (All peels and seed scoops can be gently squeezed to extract the extra juice for cooking.)

Place pears and water in a wide pot with a tiny pinch of sea salt and bring to boil.

Turn down the flame and simmer with lid on for 5 to 8 minutes, depending on ripeness of the fruit.

Meanwhile, mix the kuzu with a little cold water to dissolve.

Add the rice syrup to pears and cook for 1/2 minute.

Add the kuzu, stirring to prevent lumps, and simmer for 1 minute.

Place 1 or 2 pear halves in each bowl, then pour a little of the sauce over the top.

Sprinkle or grate a little cinnamon over the pears and cool down.

Garnish with a sprig of fresh mint or a wild flower.

A delicious vegan cream topping can be made using homemade blanched, pureed almond cream, and amasake or maple syrup to taste.

Homemade amazake

I am including this recipe because, even though the incubation time is long (8 to 12 hours), it is one of the most simply delicious pudding/dessert/sweeteners ever invented by humans. In addition, it keeps well and can be happily frozen.

Ingredients:
3 cups of sweet, short-grain brown rice
6 cups of filtered water.
1 1/2 cup of rice koji starter
a pinch of sea salt

Preparation:
Rinse and soak the rice in 6 cups of water overnight.

Bring rice to boil in heavy stainless-steel or ceramic pan and simmer with lid on for 1 hour.

Allow to cool just enough that you can hold the pot comfortably without burning your hand.

Gently mix in the koji thoroughly and replace lid.

Wrap in blankets and place in a warm, sunny spot (my new batch is in the car right now because it's toasty in there) for 8 to 12 hours or put into pilot-lit oven.

Stir the rice a couple of times and check that it is staying nice and warm.

When rice is a sweet slurry, bring to boil with a pinch of sea salt to stop the fermentation process and simmer for a minute.

Blend amazake, pour into quart mason jars, seal, and refrigerate when cooled.

You can make up a batch of drinkable amazake by blending 1 cup with 1 cup boiled water and a pinch of orange or lemon zest or a few drops of ginger juice.

Amazake also makes a satisfying rich base sweeter in almost any dessert/pudding recipe.

Regular short- or medium-grain brown rice can be used. I have experimented making amazake with 1/2 rice and 1/2 (or exclusively) with millet, whole oats, corn grits, and kamut. And they are all simply delicious. I especially like the rice/corn grits and the rice/oat groats combos.

Amazake, once bottled and sealed, can last for weeks, even months, in the fridge. And I often freeze some, which comes in handy for trips/travel.

Tips when eating out.

Soups are usually too salty, so we can order a pot/mug hot water so it can be diluted to be less so. We can ask for oatmeal to be prepared without milk or salt—i.e., plain cooked with water—and for vegetables to be plain steamed without butter. We can request dairy to be replaced with olive oil. It's helpful to plan ahead and ask for extra side dishes or portions if needed for upcoming meals when what might be available is unknown. I actually sometimes say yes to a vegan meal/snack that I am offered when flying because, even if I don't feel like it in the moment, it might come in handy later on or next day.

Tips for long-distance air, bus, or train travel. Even if my journey is only twenty-four hours of travel, I precook food to last for approximately three to four days of travel and store them in four-ounce and eight-ounce plastic BPA-free containers, some of which are frozen. I always travel with my own condiments and can add what I like when needed: beans, seaweed, and braised veggies (onion) dishes and pureed soup all freeze well. And they go into the bottom area of my rolling double-insulated Coleman cooler bag that is almost the exact size of a carry-on bag and which fits neatly into the overhead compartment on most flights. (The exception being on small commuter planes, when we are required to check it in just before boarding, when I pull out my *fragile* tag and request that it be handled with great care. So far so good.) Airlines allow properly frozen ice packs in carryon, so I usually place one big flat one on the very bottom and another on the very top before closing the zipper. Once all the frozen containers are in, I then continue to pack the cooler with a variety of cooked grains and vegetable and salad dishes along with snacks, bread, and tahini / peanut butter. There can't be any room for movement of items once packed, so I will sometimes take a 1/2 loaf sourdough bread to create a tight fit. I am always amazed at how well my food travels and most often arrive with no spills or spoilage. If I have to stay in a hotel, I can refreeze the ice packs and use containers of ice cubes to help keep food cold enough.

Questions and Answers

Question. What is the gift of this whole experience?

Answer. I can't put it into one word or idea. Humility is big on the list. Awareness. This has changed over time. Now I can safely say that I've been given the gift of knowing/getting to know myself and from this, the gift of knowing others. I've developed a modest consultation and cooking practice, the macrobiotic pantry, and enjoy supporting anyone who is at all interested in applying the simple lifestyle and dietary practices that I believe, through thirty-two years of experience, can help folks move in a direction of greater health and happiness in all ways.

Question. How do I define/understand macrobiotics?

Answer. My definition of macrobiotics is all things considered. A big, whole, inclusive life.

My feeling is that eating macrobiotically is an honest way to eat and nourish my body. In giving my attention to eating in this way, I feel I am in a state of grace and am filled with wonder and greater gratitude for all.

Question. What is the main benefit I have garnered from macrobiotics?

Answer. Knowing myself, gratitude.

Question. What is illness? What is health? Is health synonymous with happiness?

Answer. Illness is an ignorance of condition and a state of imbalance. Health is either good/balanced or poor/imbalanced. I think the question of whether health is synonymous with happiness can be switched around to ask, "Is happiness synonymous with health?" One can be happy without necessarily having a condition of good health, but the actuality of being in a state of happiness seems to me to be a healthy condition.

Question. What do I understand as the main cause of my illness?

Answer. Compromised pancreas and spleen function from birth. During her pregnancy with me, (and throughout her whole life), my mother's diet consisted of a large quantity of eggs, chicken, butter, and cheese. These foods had a very contracting effect on my pancreas spleen, and I was too tight to eat when born. Once I was offered the very rich cow's milk formula laced with sugar, I began to eat and the life cycle of hypoglycemia was triggered.

Ancestral ingestion over the years of large amounts of rich animal foods and refined sugar.

Question. How did I / does one heal?

Answer. I think the seed of health was planted when I was first introduced to macrobiotics and began eating consciously. By the time I had my first consultation with Denny Waxman, I had reached a place of such emptiness / not knowing / ignorance / surrender that I was then ready to accept and be filled with truth and wisdom and new health.

Question. Why doesn't everyone heal?

Answer. I think it's not so easy to answer this. Humans can be strong, stubborn, stoic, brave, gullible, so many different traits that when combined with pathology can be overbearing/overwhelming to deal with.

Question. How do you change / let go?

Answer. It's a lot easier to gather and accumulate than it is to get rid of / let it go. In all ways, you eat foods that build up and get stored as excess and then go on a diet to try and get rid of it. You buy things that hardly get used and then it's difficult to sell or get rid of them. I will say that probably one of the most helpful ingredients in helping us to let go or change is relaxation, massage, sweet vegetable and fresh juiced drinks, and plenty of delicious, sweet-tasting, quality vegetable foods plus a large amount of validation, empathy, and compassion.

Question. How do I participate these days in the macrobiotic community?

Answer. I have a group of close friends with whom I exchange new ideas and fresh food dishes. I give consultations when asked. I give classes and talks when the voice within speaks to do so.

Question. Is macrobiotics for everyone?

Answer. I cannot imagine that any single being on the planet would not be positively helped by eating a diet that was tailored to their unique and individual condition/needs. However, human conditions can be tricky.

Question. Do I use additional healing modalities?

Answer. I incorporate various healing modalities in any given time. I seek shiatsu, acupuncture treatments, and Chinese herbal teas when needed. I am drawn to various essential oils at various times. I request Western medical opinion and diagnosis to broaden my understanding of my state of health at various times. My interpretation of macrobiotics is all things considered.

Footnote

As I write this footnote, the world is still dealing with the COVID-19 pandemic. I am reminded of something my grandmother often repeated. She used to say she was glad that she had experienced living through two world wars because the crisis brought people together for the common good. I will add to that and say that the basic tendency for humans in crisis is to survive, and often, that can be a wake-up call to trying something new and putting old ways aside to work together for the common good for all. I can speak this from experience.

In addition, I am becoming increasingly aware that life on this planet is really rather fragile and at any moment, we could all be facing a different kind of world disaster, such as the tectonic plates shifting and our current pandemic. With this in mind, I am being prepared by making sure I have plenty of dried, organic bulk grains, beans, and specialty foods. I do not fear death in itself but do fear not having a say or some control in how and where I take my last breath.

I pray that I will be able to continue feeding myself and sharing with others for as long as I am in my body and when my time to depart arrives, that I will be in a beautiful natural setting steeped in nature. It is my intention to be aware when this happens. Time will tell.

Acknowledgments

Even though I probably haven't adequately stated it, I have huge gratitude and complete empathy and understanding regarding my grandmother's, mother's, and father's conditions—a revelation which occurred almost overnight after the first time I saw my macrobiotic senior counselor. At that time, I was brought to my knees in humility and felt immense gratitude to my parents.

The very fact that my grandmother took all four of her youngest daughter's children, her grandchildren, into her home to love and care for in the best possible ways she knew is surely a testament to her openhearted generosity.

I bear my parents and ancestors zero malice or blame for the parts they played in my birth condition. It simply was and is the manifestation of a long line of a certain way of eating and living and environmental habits of which they were unaware and that which, until the moment of realization that I was given to see what I had been born with, had gone unaddressed.

I thank all my ancestors, grandparents, parents, and siblings for gifting me with life and giving me such an extraordinary life start, experiences, and opportunities to share and work through my stuff and become more myself.

To Rosie, thank you for choosing me to be your birth mother. You are, without a doubt, the most special and significant person in my life, and I thank you and your dear husband for gifting me anew with a precious and most delightful grandboy!

To Mourka and Miklos, Chana, Bob and Joshua, Nancy and family, Margie and Jeff, Tom, Rene, Angelo, Helen, Stacy, Francesca and Charles, your love and support keep expanding the meaning of friendship. There really aren't adequate words to express my gratitude.

To Angel and Nadia, you stepped in, nurtured, and supported me at such a crucial time in my life. I love you and am forever grateful.

Saying thank-you seems an insufficient way of telling all the dear friends, teachers, therapists, makers, and suppliers of wonderful, organic, high-quality foods and all those who have both supported, encouraged, and helped me on my journey. I am forever grateful and feel great love for you all.

Throughout each and every day, I am reminded that I am surrounded with items that fellow humans have imagined, created, and manufactured to support me in the gift of living: cars, sofas, beds, clothing, cooking utensils, windows, roads, bridges, computers, telephones, toothbrushes, bowls, doorknobs, books, light bulbs. The list is endless! Thank you to each and every one of you.

For all the wonderful music, poetry, and art that stimulates, soothes, uplifts, inspires, I thank you all, both deceased and still living, for sharing your great artistic gifts.

It seems that the years spent in the company and caring for the elderly relatives during my childhood well prepared me for the role I would eventually play in the lives of several elder friends over the years since I recovered. I am truly grateful, especially for the friendship and opportunity of caring for three special women who enriched my life and whom have all left this earthly world a sweeter place for them having lived.

Rosemary Stark was a gem of a person with the most wonderful sense of humor. Thank you, Rosemary, for thirty years of sharing in so many ways.

Etti Reed was a beautiful soul who became my first client on Maui when I started a macrobiotic cooking and consulting business in 2002.

Adele Golub was such a dear special person—the mother of my partner, Evan, with whom I spent many wonderful times, especially in her last years of life in Maui, Hawaii.

What great fortune was bestowed on me by meeting Harry Hart and Loretta Quartey, who introduced me to the concept of a macrobiotic way of living in such a generous and believable way because of who they were. They played such a vital role in changing my destiny, and I am so very grateful to them forever.

I have had an extra thirty-two years on this earth, thanks to being guided to seeking the consul and following the recommendations of Denny Waxman. I am eternally grateful to him for sharing his wisdom with me during a critical time in my life and continuously supporting my highest state of health and well-being through his strengthening health program. I feel humbled and honored to know you.

Denny Waxman

SHI (Strengthening Health Institute)

(215) 271-1858

A special thank-you to the friends and members of the Ulster County LETS who rallied to help build my cabin they endearingly called the Taj Mahal. It is the sweetest place on the planet that I am fortunate to be able to call home.

Thank you Ben for helping create an extraordinary and beautiful daughter.

To Evan, for all the ups and downs, thank you for caring and adding many rich and complex layers to my journey.

And finally, to Laura Shaine Cunningham and all at Fulton Books for getting the manuscript print-ready and published....you miraculously turned my attempt at telling a story into a legible book! Thank you. What a gift!

Portrait of myself, summer of 1966, age nine years

Christmas photograph of myself (back row, far right) and siblings
on the front staircase at St. Nicholas, 1965 The portrait in the
background is of MM done in 1906 when she was five years old.

St. Nicholas, the home of my maternal grandparents
and my home from the age of four years, 1961

MM, mummy's mummy on her favorite seat on
the border of St. Nicholas gardens.

My mother in the garden at St. Nicholas, summer 1993

With Rose age two months, 1978

With Rose, age seven months

Taken soon after the move to Florida, 1980

The old cow shed in the rock garden at St. Nicholas—
my retreat home for four months in 1989

With Rose in Sarasota, Florida, Christmas 1990

The cabin project begins, October 1996

In front of the cottage I rented on Maui, Hawaii, in 2001

The finished cabin made from all recycled, donated, and found materials

Well pump cover

Rainwater catchment system, 2021

Food jars in the cabin kitchen area

Prayerful nook in the cabin

First raised-bed garden, 2021

Beautiful bounty from the garden, 2021

The sweetest carrots I ever tasted!

Blanched salad with Nappa cabbage, cauliflower, and scallions

Beautiful visitor to the land

About the Author

 Christina was born and educated in North Yorkshire, England. She met and married an American who was living in London, and they moved to the United States with their baby daughter in 1979.

It is probably not an accident that Christina has been so interested in food and health for much of her sixty-four years on the planet.

Born not wanting to eat, health-compromised, and struggling in her body for most of her childhood, then flirting with death both consciously and unconsciously, Christina was eventually and most fortunately guided to a whole new way of living and eating that has gifted her ever since with an abundance of great good health, humility, and gratitude for all.

She has had a very diversified career as a chef with a great variety of styles, transitioning from cordon bleu to macrobiotics. Christina also enjoys designing clothing, is a gifted seamstress, and has assisted in a few different national and international aid programs.

Christina now resides in the lower Catskill Mountains in Upstate New York in a beautiful recycled wood cabin that she built with the help of some very generous friends involved in the community barter system that she set up in 1996. She has a strong connection to and love of nature and all that is natural and strives to tread gently on the earth.

www.cookprayeat.org

Lightning Source UK Ltd.
Milton Keynes UK
UKHW010625121222
413785UK00002B/150